Ernest Alfred Wallis Budge

An Egyptian Reading Book

Ernest Alfred Wallis Budge

An Egyptian Reading Book

ISBN/EAN: 9783337330293

Printed in Europe, USA, Canada, Australia, Japan

Cover: Foto ©Thomas Meinert / pixelio.de

More available books at **www.hansebooks.com**

AN

EGYPTIAN READING BOOK.

COMPILED BY

E. A. WALLIS BUDGE, M.A.

ASSISTANT IN THE DEPARTMENT OF EGYPTIAN AND ASSYRIAN ANTIQUITIES, BRITISH MUSEUM.

LONDON:
D. NUTT, 270, STRAND.

1888.

HARRISON AND SONS,
PRINTERS IN ORDINARY TO HER MAJESTY,
ST. MARTIN'S LANE, LONDON.

TO

MAJOR-GEN. SIR HENRY CRESWICKE RAWLINSON,

K.C.B., F.R.S., D.C.L., LL.D

ETC., ETC.

PREFACE.

FOR some years past it has been the custom of Mr. F. G. Hilton Price, F.S.A., to invite to his house at regular intervals a small number of students and others interested in the language and archæology of ancient Egypt for the systematic study of the same. Four winters ago I was invited by him to join this little class, and, assuming that each member was well acquainted with Mr. Renouf's *Egyptian Grammar*,* and the lists of hieroglyphic signs as published by the late Dr. Birch,† E. de Rougé,‡ and Dr. H. Brugsch,§ the study of the well known story of the *Tale of the Two Brothers* was commenced. At that time no complete hieroglyphic transcript of this text existed to my knowledge, and I transcribed the hieratic text into hieroglyphics for our use. This text was chosen for study because there are many easy passages in it, and because it is nearly complete, and the interesting nature of this ancient story makes it pleasant reading for students. Towards the close of the year 1886 Mr. Hilton Price suggested that this tran-

* *An Elementary Grammar of the Ancient Egyptian Language in the Hieroglyphic type*, by P. le Page Renouf.

† Bunsen, *Egypt's Place in Universal History*, I.

‡ E. de Rougé, *Chrestomathie*, 1er fascicule.

§ *Verzeichniss der Hieroglyphen.*

script, together with a few others of complete compositions, should be published; but my mission to Egypt in that year prevented this suggestion from taking a practical form. In the following year, having discussed his suggestion more fully, Mr. Hilton Price again urged forward the matter: but at the outset we were stopped by the cost of printing the proposed book of hieroglyphic texts. In this difficulty he appealed to a few personal friends for assistance, and it is entirely owing to the liberality of the following ladies and gentlemen that it has been possible for this book to appear.

MISS H. M. ADAIR.
ALFRED AMES, ESQ.
W. A. TYSSEN AMHERST, ESQ., M.P.
MRS. TYSSEN AMHERST.
FREDERICK ELLIOT BLACKSTONE, B.C.L.
JOHN CLAYTON, ESQ., F.S.A.
MISS CLENDINING.
WILLIAM YOUNGER FLETCHER, ESQ., F.S.A.
MRS. GOODISON.
G. GUNNING, ESQ.
H. RIDER HAGGARD, ESQ.
CHARLES HARRISON, ESQ., F.S.A.
JESSE HAWORTH, ESQ.
THE REV. W. L. LAWSON, M.A.
F. CLAUGHTON MATTHEWS, M.A.
F. D. MOCATTA, ESQ.
WALTER MORRISON, ESQ.
SIR CHARLES NICHOLSON, BART.
F. G. HILTON PRICE, ESQ., F.S.A.
SIR HENRY RAWLINSON, K.C.B.
LORD ARTHUR RUSSELL.
E. MAUNDE THOMPSON, ESQ., F.S.A.
E. TOWRY WHYTE, ESQ., M.A.

The greater number of the texts printed in this book are transcribed from the hieratic, and some of these, such as the *Festival Songs of Isis and Nephthys*, the *Litanies of Seker*, and the extracts from the great Harris Papyrus, are published for the first time. About one hundred and fifty pages of this book contain transcripts from hieratic texts: these may be useful to those who study this difficult branch of Egyptology for the first time. No pains have been spared to make the transcriptions as accurate and uniform as possible. I have, of course, made use of the transcripts of other workers wherever they existed, but in all cases, where the papyri transcribed by them belonged to the Trustees of the British Museum, I collated them afresh. Every text in this book is complete except the extracts from the Annals of Rameses III (Harris Papyrus, No. 1, Brit. Mus., No. 9999). It would have been impossible to print a transcript of the whole text inscribed upon the 133 feet of this magnificent papyrus in a small book like this, and it was therefore decided to excerpt the first and last sections, which are complete in themselves, from it. In the table of contents references have been given to the books in which translations of the texts given in the following pages have been published, and where reproductions of the hieratic and hieroglyphic texts have been made. It has not been thought necessary to add a list of hieroglyphic signs, as the *Verzeichniss* of Dr. Brugsch is cheap and easily accessible. A complete vocabulary and transliterations of the texts would have been useful adjuncts to this book, but the cost of printing does not allow of this work being undertaken at present.

The typographical part of this work has been executed by Messrs. Harrison and Sons with their usual excellence, and their compositors, Messrs. Fisher and Smith, have performed their task most creditably.

E. A. WALLIS BUDGE.

October, 1888.

CONTENTS.

PAGES

I. THE TALE OF THE TWO BROTHERS. 1–25

Transcript into hieroglyphics from the hieratic text of the British Museum papyrus (D'Orbiney) No. 10183. The hieratic text has been published by Birch, *Select Papyri*, II, plates ix–xix; Moldenke, *The Tale of the Two Brothers* (printed in the Leyden hieratic type); and by Reinisch, *Aegyptische Chrestomathie*, Taf. 22–40. Since the transcript in this book was printed off in Nov., 1887, a transcript by M. Groff (*Étude sur le Papyrus d'Orbiney*, Paris, 1888) has appeared. The text of this story was analysed and discussed by M. de Rougé in the *Revue Archéologique*, tom. ix, p. 385, and by Goodwin in his *Cambridge Essays*, p. 382 ff. Translations of the text have been made by Dr. Brugsch (*Aus dem Orient*, p. 7 ff.), by M. Maspero (*Revue Arch.*, N.S., t. xxxv, pp. 164–179), and by Mr. Renouf (*Records of the Past*, ii, p. 137 ff.). The first six pages of this papyrus were transcribed into English letters and published by Mr. Renouf in the *Atlantis*, vol. iv, 1863, pp. 23–57, as a proof of the scientific accuracy of the method of Egyptian decipherment then current among the best Egyptologists.

II. THE POSSESSED PRINCESS OF BEχTEN. 26–30

This text has been published by Rosellini, *Monumenti Storici*, ii, pl. 48; by De Rougé, *Journal Asiatique*, 5 série, t. viii, pp. 201–248; t. x, pp. 112–168; t. xi, pp. 509–572; t. xii, pp. 221–270; and by Prisse, *Monuments Égyptiens*, pl. 24. Dr. Erman has proved (*Aeg. Zeit.*, 1883, pp. 54–60) that this composition is a legend written for the purpose of glorifying the god Chensu long after the period to which it purports to belong. For an English translation see *Records of the Past*, iv, pp. 53–60.

PAGES

III. The Festival Songs of Isis and Nephthys. 30–45

Transcript into hieroglyphics from the hieratic text of the first composition in the British Museum papyrus No. 10188. A notice of this papyrus was published by Dr. Pleyte in the *Recueil de Travaux*, iii, p. 57; he translated a few passages from it, and gave a summary of the headings of the chapters. In the *Proc. Soc. Bib. Arch.*, Nov., 1886, I published an account of it, and transcribed a few of the important passages. I hope to publish translations of the texts in this papyrus in the new edition of the *Records of the Past.*

IV. Colophon. 45, 46

This colophon states that the papyrus was written for Nesi-Åmsu, the son of Pe-ṭā-Åmen-suten-taiu, a prophet of Åmen-Rā, Horus, and the other gods of Thebes, in the 12th year of Alexander II, or about B.C. 305.

V. The Lamentations of Isis and Nephthys. 46–51

Transcript into hieroglyphics from the hieratic text of the Berlin papyrus No. 1425, published by Dr. J. de Horrack under the title *Les Lamentations d'Isis et de Nephthys.* For an English translation see *Records of the Past*, pp. ii, 117–126.

VI. The Litanies of Seker. 52–57

Transcript into hieroglyphics from the hieratic text of the second composition in the British Museum papyrus No. 10188. The second colophon printed on pp. 56, 57 contains imprecations upon any person who shall remove the papyrus from its place.

VII. The Inscription of Unȧ. 58–63

This inscription has been published by De Rougé, in his *Recherches sur les Monuments: six premières Dynasties.* A more correct edition of the text has been published by Dr. Erman in the *Aeg. Zeit.*, 1882, pp. 1–29, with an excellent literal translation and a running commentary. An English translation was published by the late Dr. Birch in *Records of the Past*, ii, pp. 3–8.

PAGES

VIII. THE INSCRIPTION OF CHNEMU-ḤETEP. 64–70

This inscription has been published by Burton, *Excerpta Hieroglyphica*, pl. xxxiii, xxxiv; Champollion, *Monuments*, t. ii, pp. 418–422; Lepsius, *Denkmäler*, ii. bl. 125, 126; Brugsch, *Monuments Égyptiens*, pl. 15–17; Reinisch, *Aegyptische Chrestomathie*, i, pl. 1–4; Maspero, *Recueil de Travaux*, i, pp. 160–169. Dr. Brugsch translated for the first time about 100 lines of this important text (*Geschichte Aegyptens*, pp. 139–143 and 149, 150); a French translation of the whole text was published by M. Maspero, *Recueil de Travaux*, i, pp. 160–169; and an English translation by Dr. Birch was published in *Records of the Past*, xii, pp. 67–76.

IX. INSCRIPTIONS ON THE BASE OF THE OBELISK OF HATSHEPSU. 70–73

This text has been published by Prisse, *Monuments*, pl. 18, and by Lepsius, *Denkmäler*, iii, pl. 22. A French translation of it was published by De Rougé in *Mélanges d'Archéologie Égyptienne et Assyrienne*, iii, p. 90, and one in English by Mr. Renouf in *Records of the Past*, xii, pp. 131–136.

X. STELÆ OF NECHT-ÅMSU. 74–78

These texts have been published by Prisse, *Monuments*, pl. 17; Sharpe, *Egyptian Inscriptions*, pl. 106; and by Lepsius, *Denkmäler*, iii, 114 *i*. One of the texts was partly translated by Dr. Brugsch in the *Deutsche Revue*, vii, p. 73, and both have been given with interlinear transliteration and translation in *Trans. Soc. Bib. Arch.*, viii, pt. 3.

PAGES

XI. THE BATTLE OF KADESH. 78–82

This text has been published by Champollion, *Monuments*, pl. xxvii–xxix; and by Lepsius, *Denkmäler*, Ab. iii, pl. 187. Translations have been published by Chabas in the *Revue Archéologique*, 1858, and by De Rougé in the *Revue Contemporaine*, 1868. The text given in this book is reprinted from the edition published by M. Paul Guieyesse in the *Recueil de Travaux*, viii, pp. 126–131.

XII. ANNALS OF RAMESES III. 82–108

Transcript into hieroglyphics from the hieratic text of the great British Museum Harris papyrus, No. 9999, plates 1–9, 20, and 75–79. The complete hieratic text was published for the Trustees of the British Museum, with an English translation by Dr. Birch, entitled *Facsimile of an Egyptian Hieratic Papyrus of the reign of Rameses III.* Translations of parts of it have been published by Eisenlohr, *Die grosse Papyrus Harris;* by Birch, *Aeg. Zeit.*, 1872, p. 119; 1873, pp. 9, 34, 65, 97, 152; by Eisenlohr, *Aeg. Zeit.*, 1873, pp. 15, 49, 98, 154; 1874, pp. 23–25; by Chabas, *Recherches pour servir à l'histoire de la XIXème Dynastie*, pp. 75–79; and by Drs. Birch and Eisenlohr in *Records of the Past*, vi, pp. 21–70; and viii, pp. 5–52. The fifteen plates which I have transcribed contain the introduction to the papyrus; one half of the account of the dedication of buildings, etc., to the gods of Thebes; and the important historical summary which concludes the papyrus. The transcript of Plate XX is inserted as a specimen of the way in which numbers are expressed in Egyptian. Dr. Karl Piehl's *Dictionnaire du Papyrus Harris No. I* will be found most useful in the study of this papyrus.

XIII. THE STELÆ OF PI-ĀNχI-MERI-ÅMEN. 108–129

This text has been published by Mariette, *Monuments Divers*, pl. 1–4, and by De Rougé in his *Chrestomathie*, fasc. iv. Translations have been published by De Rougé in his *Chrestomathie*, fasc. iv, and in *Records of the Past*, ii, pp. 73–98.

PAGES

XIV. THE DECREE OF CANOPUS. 129–137

The text of this celebrated Decree has been published by Lepsius, with transliteration and translation, in *Das bilingue Dekret von Kanopus;* and by Reinisch and Roessler, *Die zweisprachige Inschrift von San.* An English translation by Dr. Birch appeared in *Records of the Past*, vii, pp. 83–90.

XV. THE PRECEPTS OF KAḲEMNA. 138, 139

XVI. THE PRECEPTS OF PTAḤ-ḤETEP. 140–157

A facsimile of the Hieratic text of the Precepts of Kaḳemna and of Ptaḥ-Ḥetep was published by Prisse at Paris in 1847, entitled *Fac-simile d'un papyrus égyptien en caractères hiératiques.* Translations and explanations of these difficult texts have been published by Chabas in the *Revue Archéologique*, 1re Série, t. xv, and in *Bibliothèque Orientale*, t. ii, pp. 173–174; by Lauth in the *Sitzungsberichte der Königl. Bayer. Akad. der Wissen. zu München*, 1869, 1870; by Dümichen, *Les Sentences de Kakemni*, Paris, 1884, t. ii, p. 80; by Virey in his *Études sur le Papyrus Prisse*, Paris, 1887, where a transcript and new translation with notes are given; and many passages have been explained by Dr. Brugsch in the supplement to his *Wörterbuch.*

XVII. THE TRAVELS OF AN EGYPTIAN. 157–169

Transcript into hieroglyphics from the hieratic text of Brit. Mus. papyrus No. 10247, pp. 18–28. A facsimile of the hieratic was published by Dr. Birch in *Select Papyri in the Hieratic Character*, pl. 52–62, and by Chabas in *Voyage d'un Égyptien en Syrie, en Phénicie, etc.*, where it was accompanied by a copy of the hieratic text, a double transcription into hieroglyphic and Coptic characters, a French translation and a running commentary. English translations have been published by Goodwin in his *Cambridge Essays*, pp. 267–269, and in *Records of the Past*, ii, pp. 107–116.

PAGES

XVIII. HYMN TO ÅMEN-RĀ. 169–176

Transcript into hieroglyphics from the hieratic text contained in Bûlâḳ papyrus No. 17. A facsimile of the text was published by Mariette in *Les Papyrus Égyptiens du Musée de Boulaq*, t. ii, pl. 11–13, and a hieroglyphic transcript with a translation and running commentary, entitled *Hymne à Ammon-Ra*, was published by M. Grébaut. English translations have been published by Goodwin in *Trans. Soc. Bib. Arch.*, ii, p. 250 ff., and in *Records of the Past*, ii, pp. 127–136.

XIX. THE SPOLIATION OF THE TOMBS. 177–194

Transcript into hieroglyphics from the hieratic text of Brit. Mus. papyrus (Abbott) No. 10221. The hieratic text was published by Dr. Birch in *Select Papyri in the Hieratic Character*, Part II, pl. i-viii, together with a general summary of its contents. French translations have been published by Chabas in *Mélanges Égyptologiques*, 3ème serie, t. i, and by Maspero in *Une Enquête Judiciaire à Thebes au temps de la XXe Dynastie*, where an excellent transcript of this badly written text, with interlinear translation, is given. An English translation was published in *Records of the Past*, xii, pp. 103–115, by De Horrack.

THE TALE OF THE TWO BROTHERS.

6.
7.
8.
2 inches broken.
9.
(?)
10.
II. 1.
(?)
2.

¾ inch broken.
3.
4.
5.
(?)
6.
7.
1½ inch broken.
8.
9.
10.
III. 1.

2.
3.
4.
5.
(sic)
6.
4 inches broken.
7.
8.

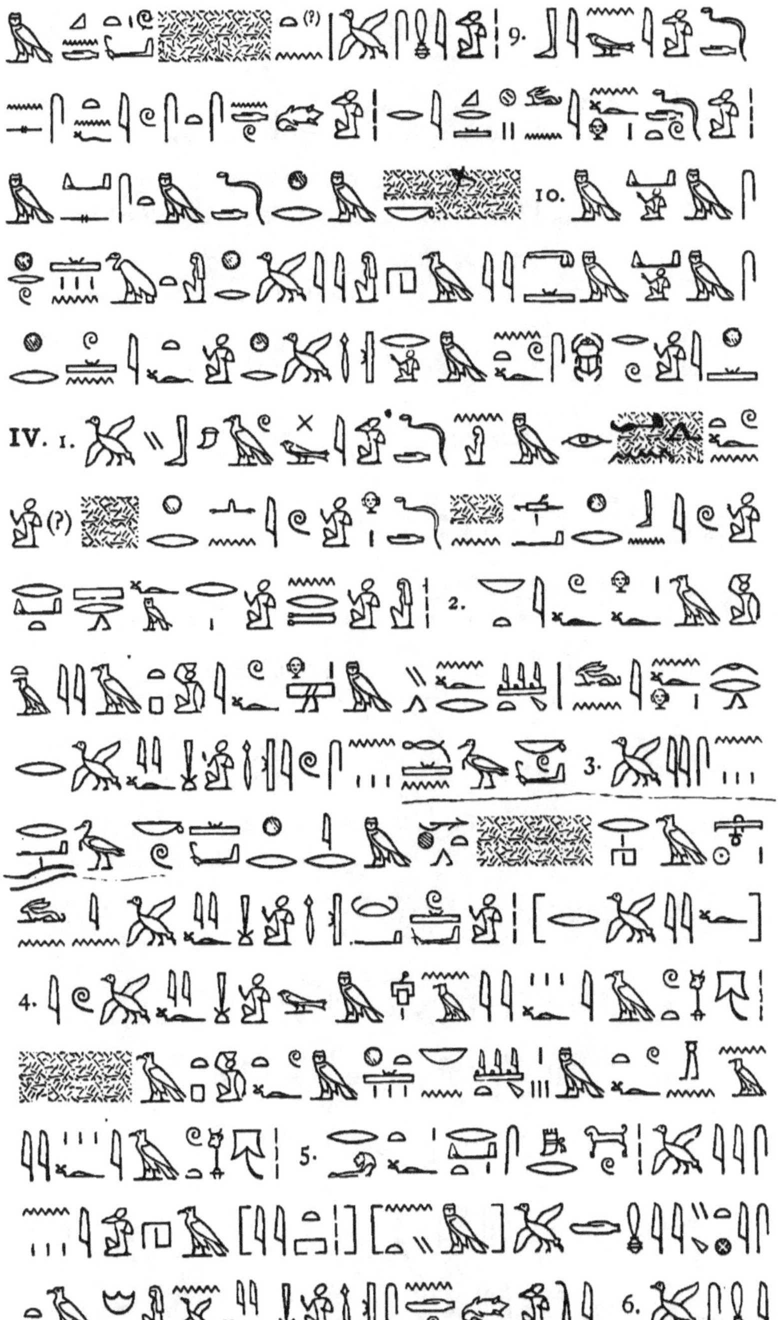

7.
8.
9.
10.
V. 1.
2.

3.
4.
5.
6.
7.
8.
9.

* The papyrus actually has here 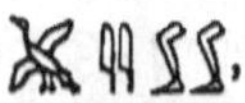, but the last two signs , have been written by a modern hand.

† The papyrus actually has 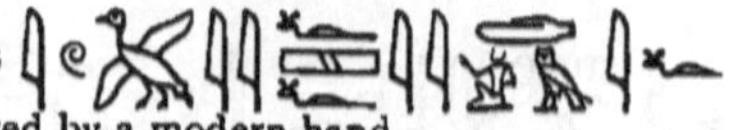 The last nine characters have been altered by a modern hand.

* Here the writing has been altered by a modern hand.

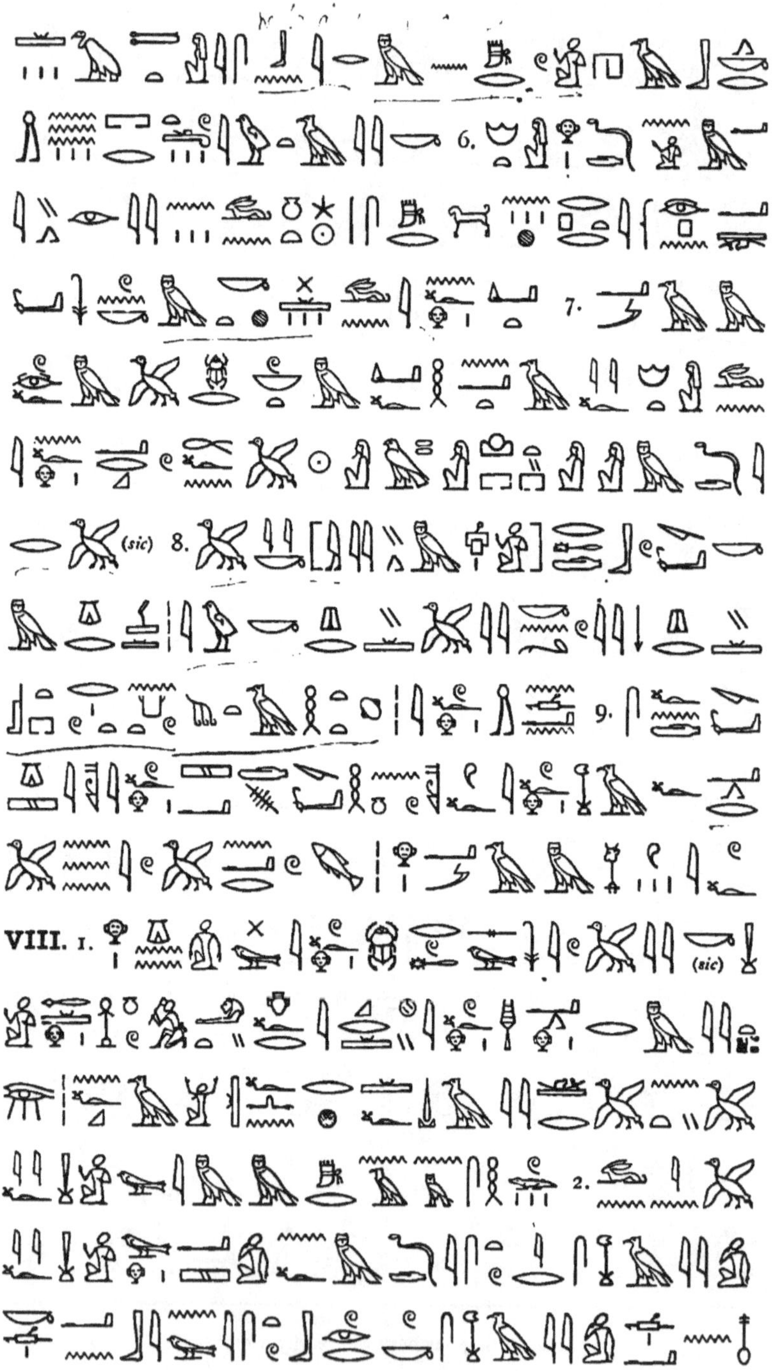
6.
7.
(sic)
8.
9.
VIII. 1.
(sic)
2.

3.
4.
5.
sic)
6.
7.

8.

9.

IX. 1.

2.

3.

4.

5.
6.
7.
8.
9.
X. 1.
2.
3.

XI. 1.
2.
3.
4.
5.
6.
7.

8.
9.
10.
XII. 1.
2.
3.
4.
5.

* The papyrus has here .

* The papyrus has here been altered by a later hand.

* The papyrus has here been altered by a later hand.

8.
9.
10.
XVII. 1.
2.
3.
4.
5.

* Some words appear to have been left out here by the scribe.

2.
3.
4.
5.
(sic.)
2 inches illegible
6.
7.
(?)
8.
9.
10.
(sic)
XIX. 1.

* Supplied from line 6.

THE POSSESSED PRINCESS OF BEXTEN.

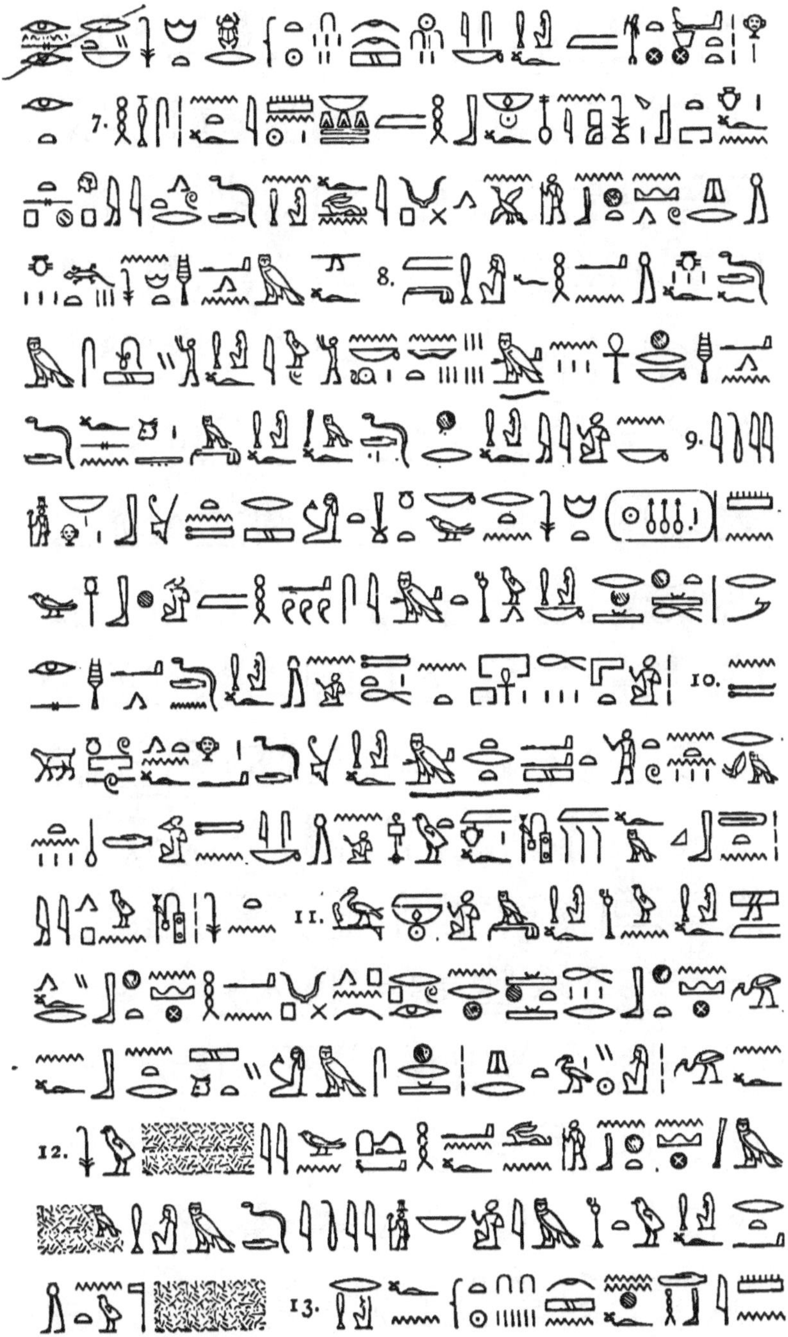

14.
15.
16.
17.
18.
19.

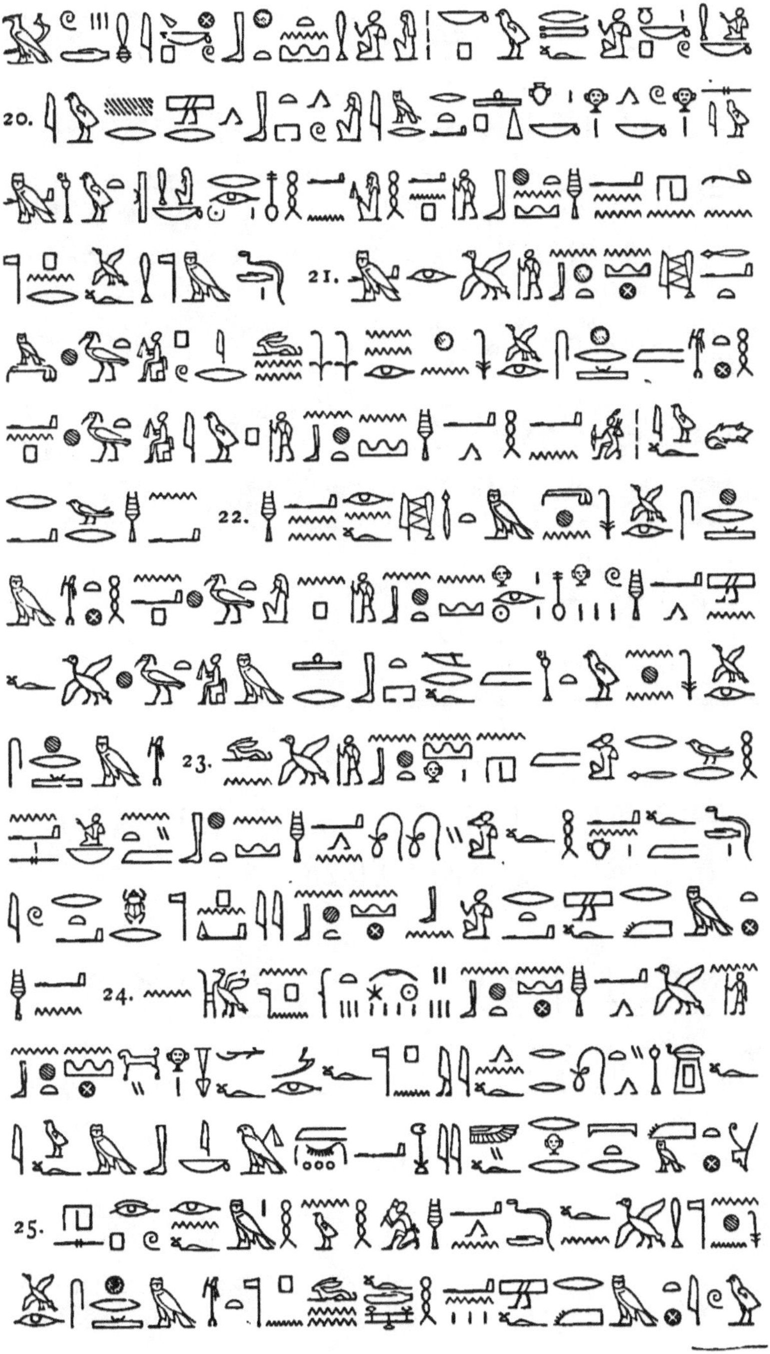
20.
21.
22.
23.
24.
25.

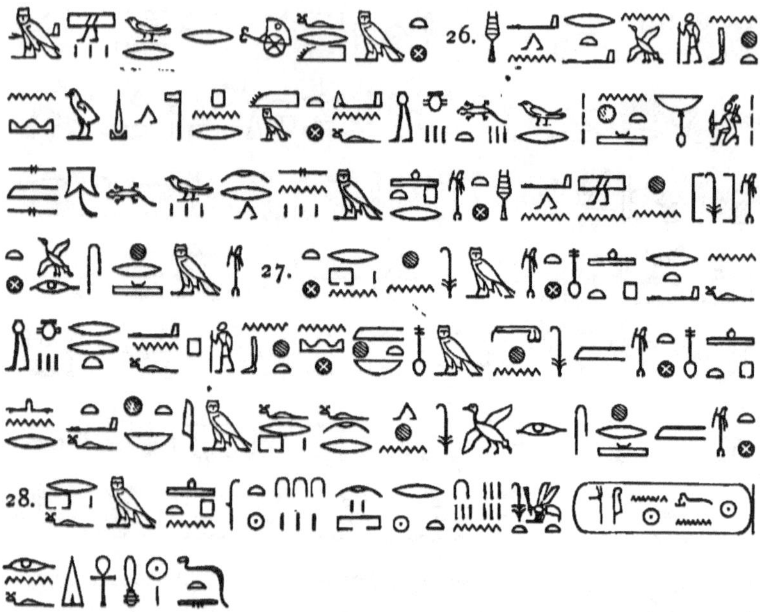

THE FESTIVAL SONGS OF ISIS AND NEPHTHYS.

1¾ inch broken
II.

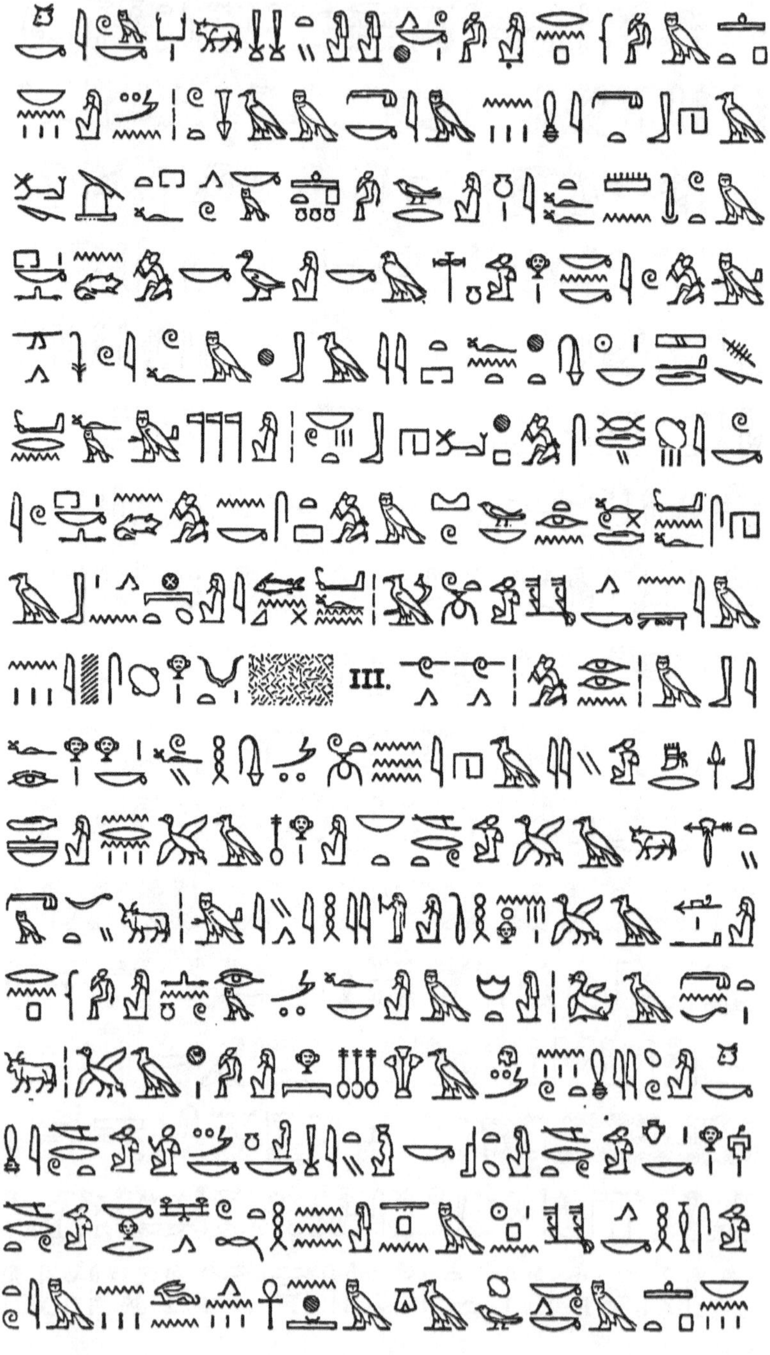
III.

E

V.

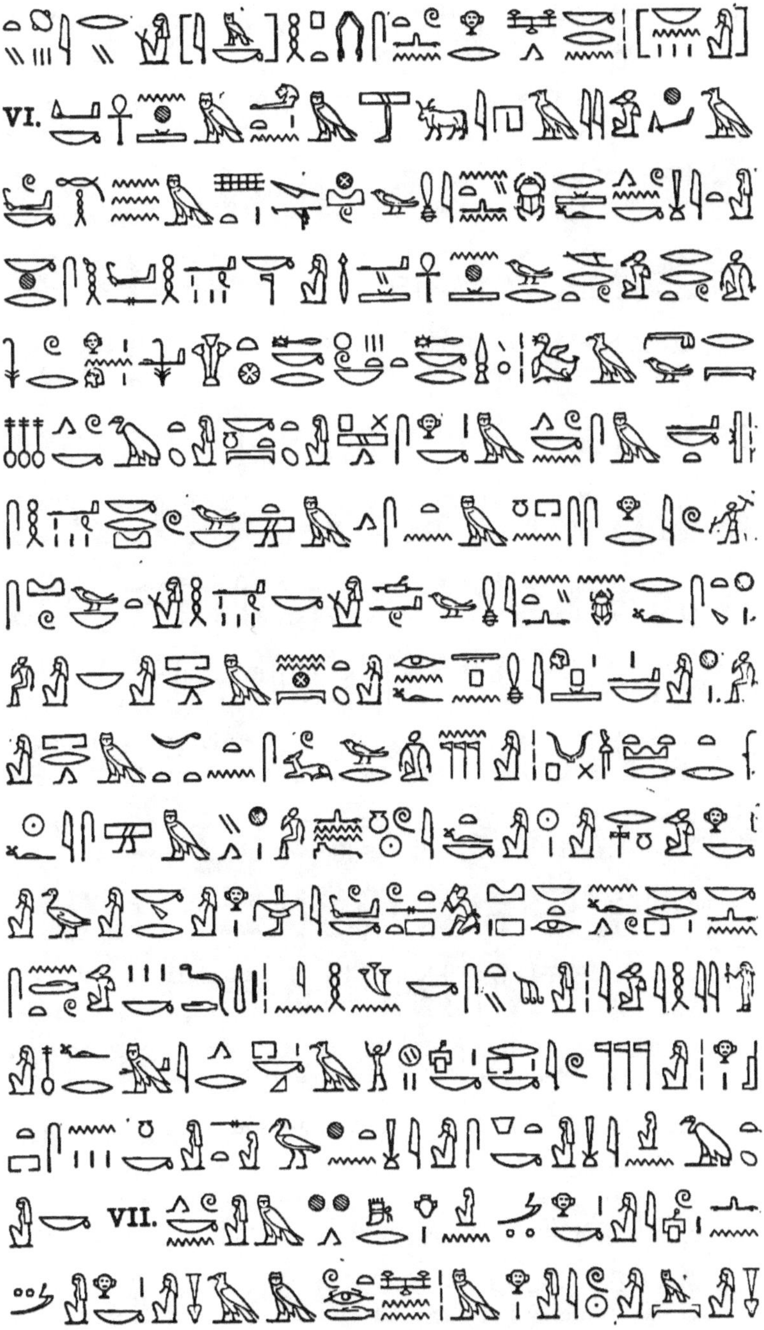
VI.
VII.

VIII.

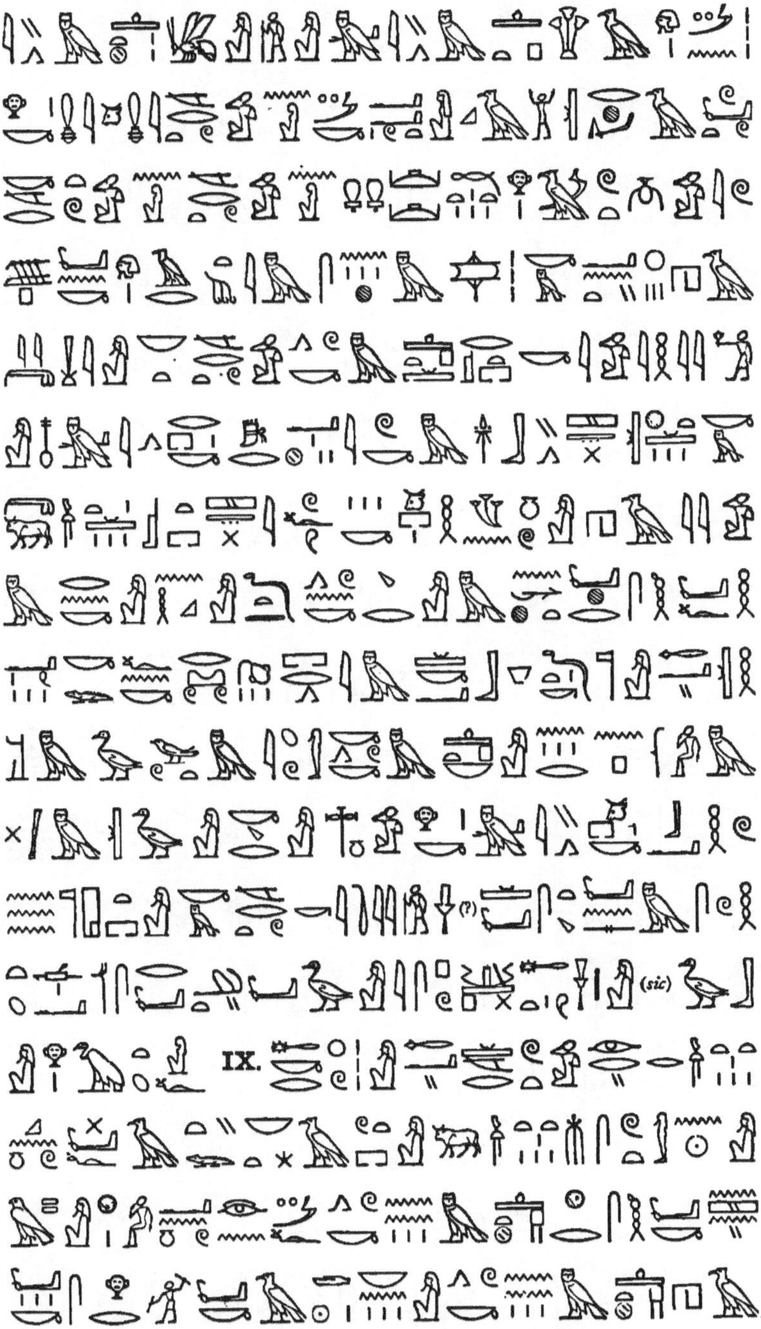
(?)
(sic)
IX.

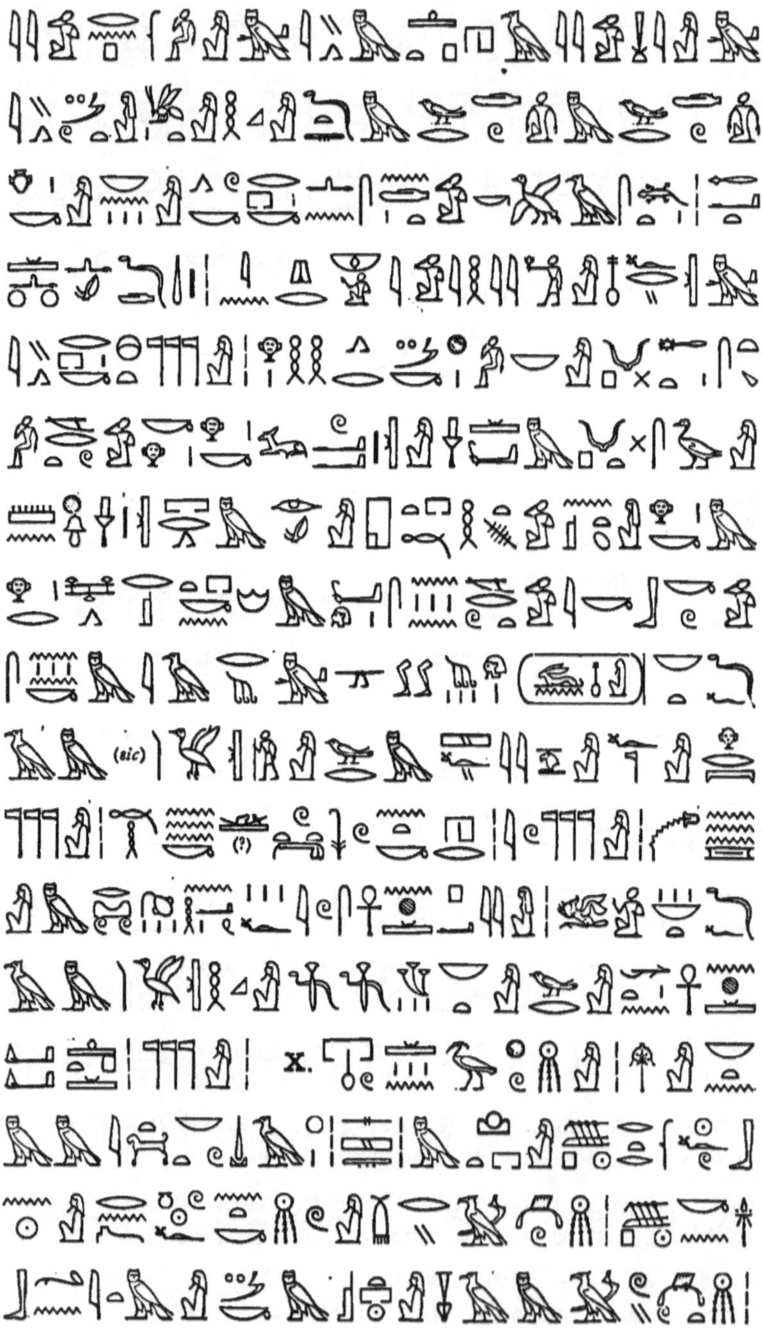
(sic)
(?)
X.

(?)
XI.
(sic)
(sic)
(sic)

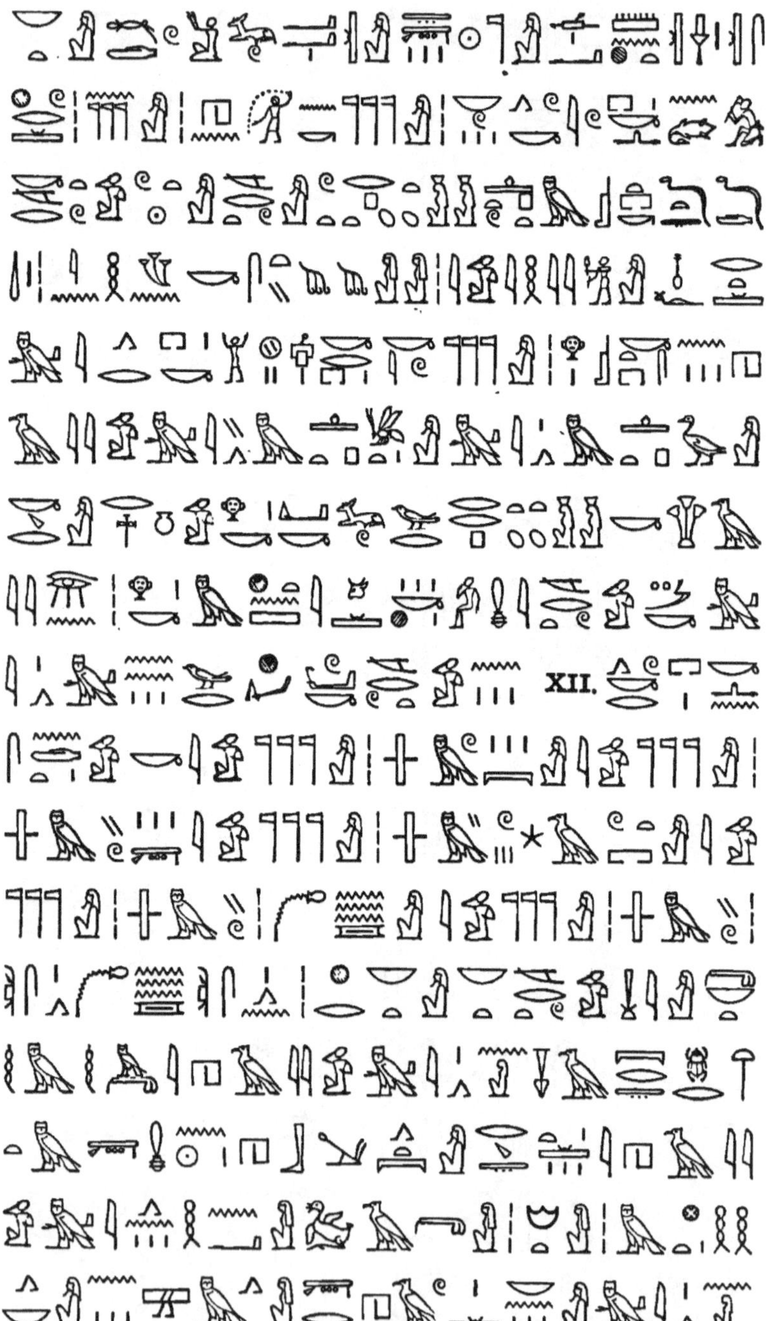
XII.

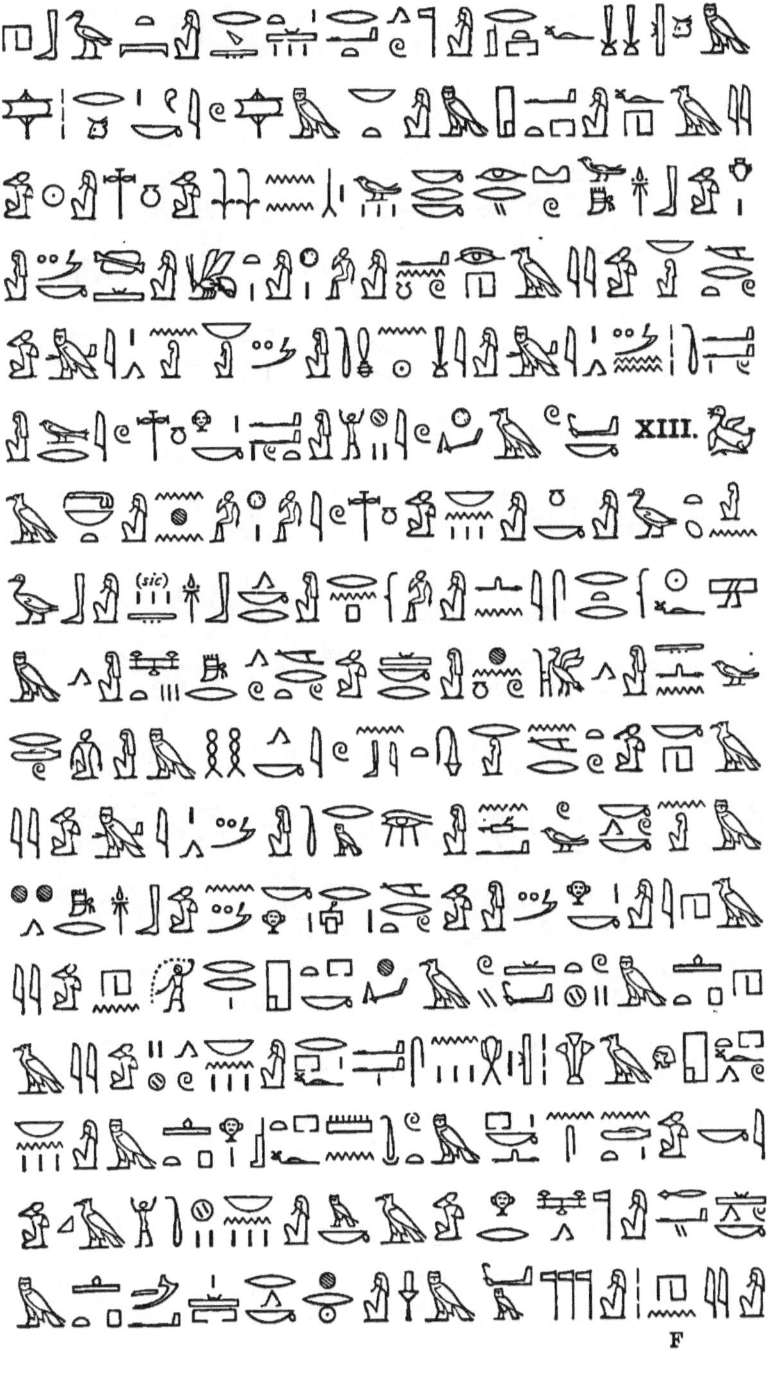
XIII.
(sic)

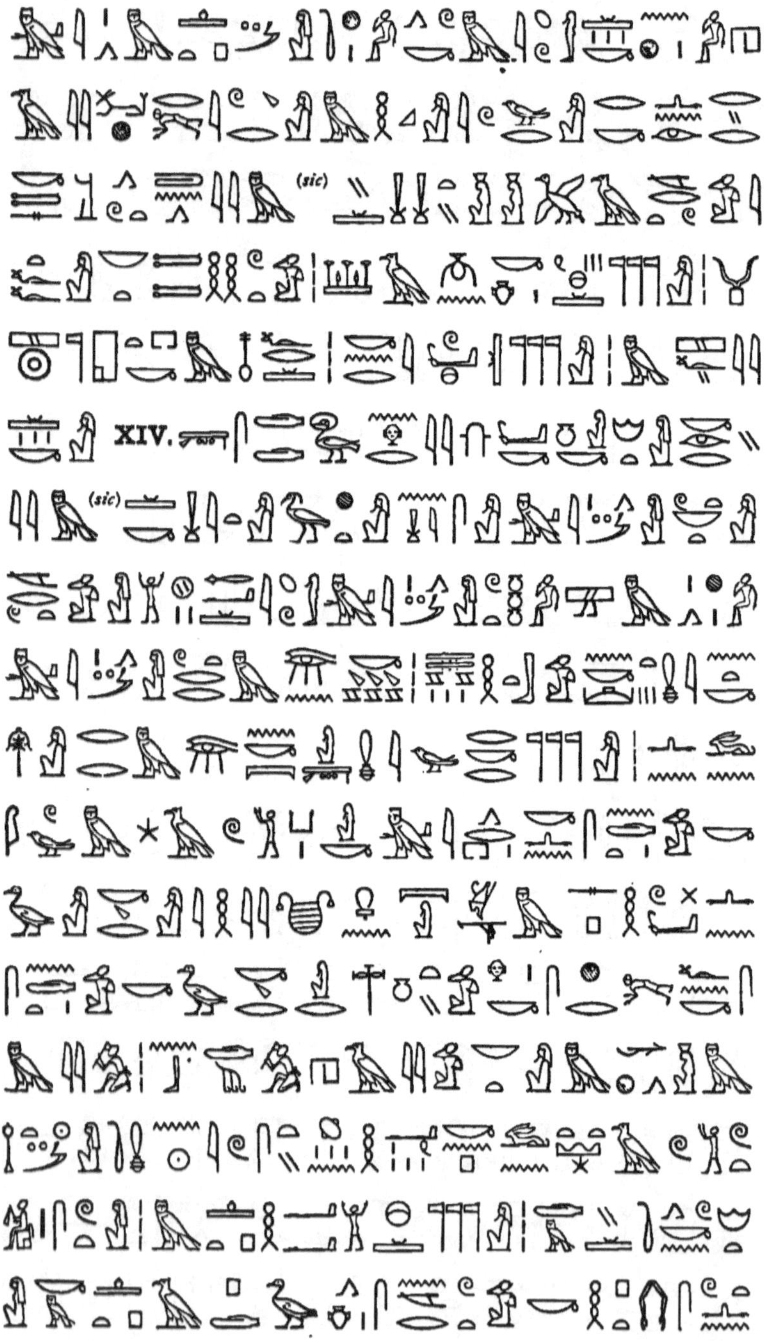
(sic)
XIV.
(sic)

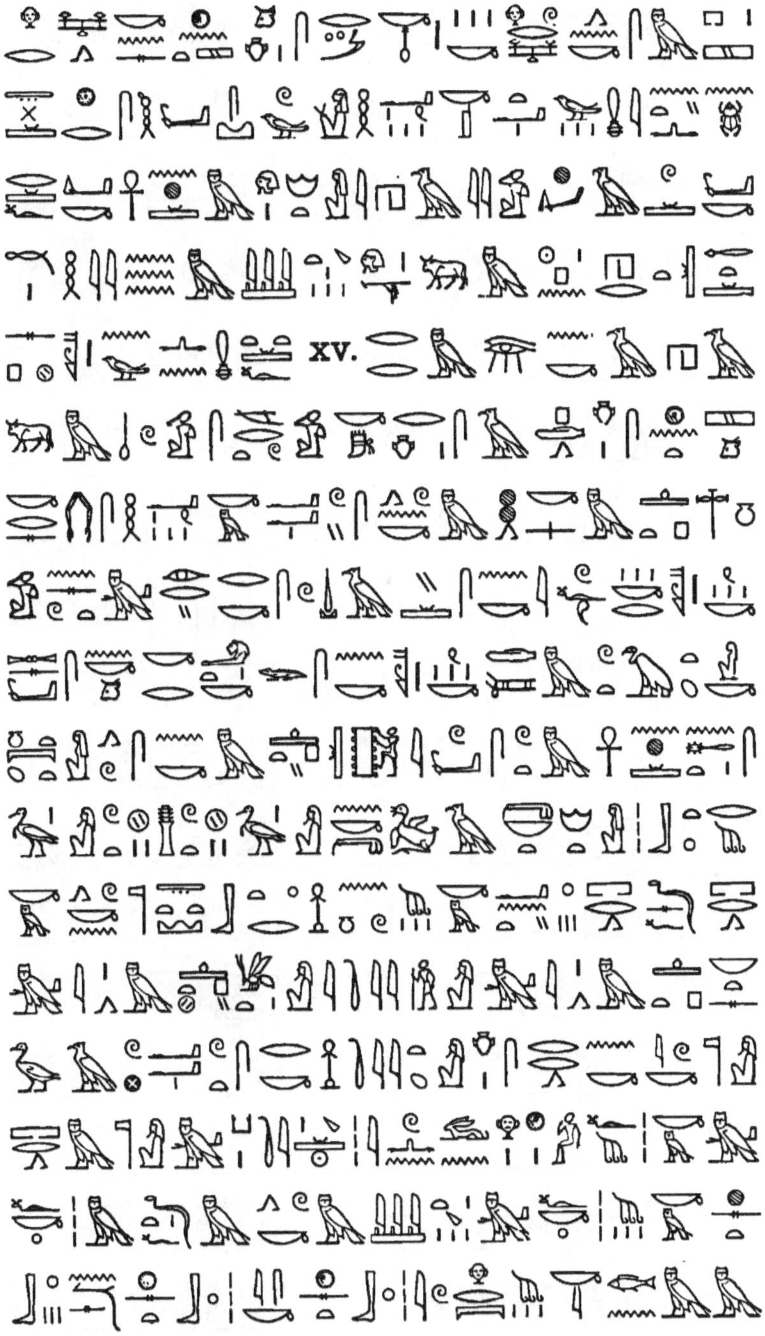
XV.

XVI.

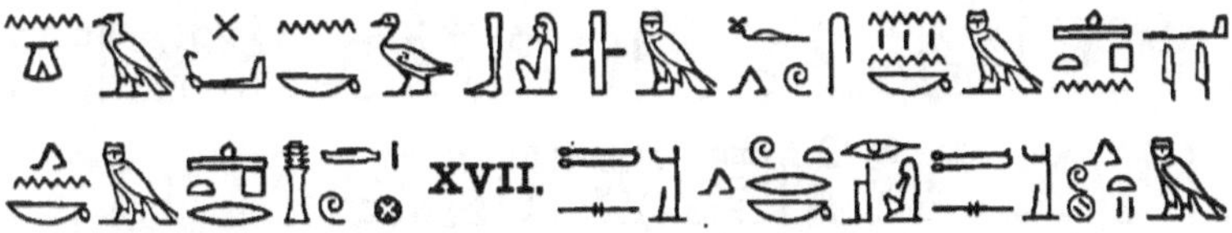

XVII.

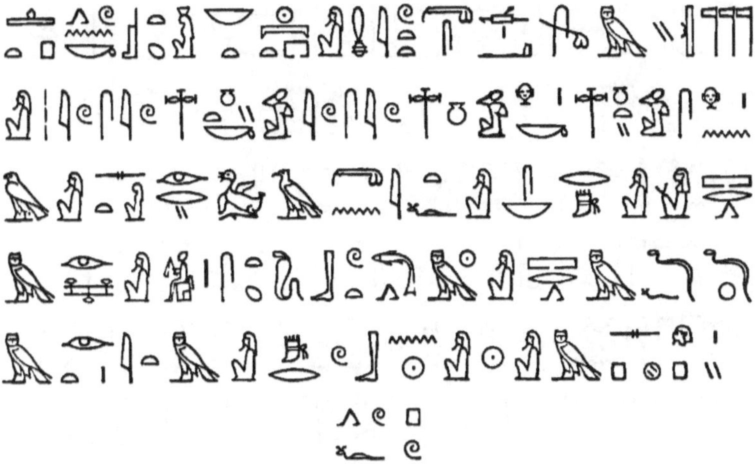

COLOPHON.

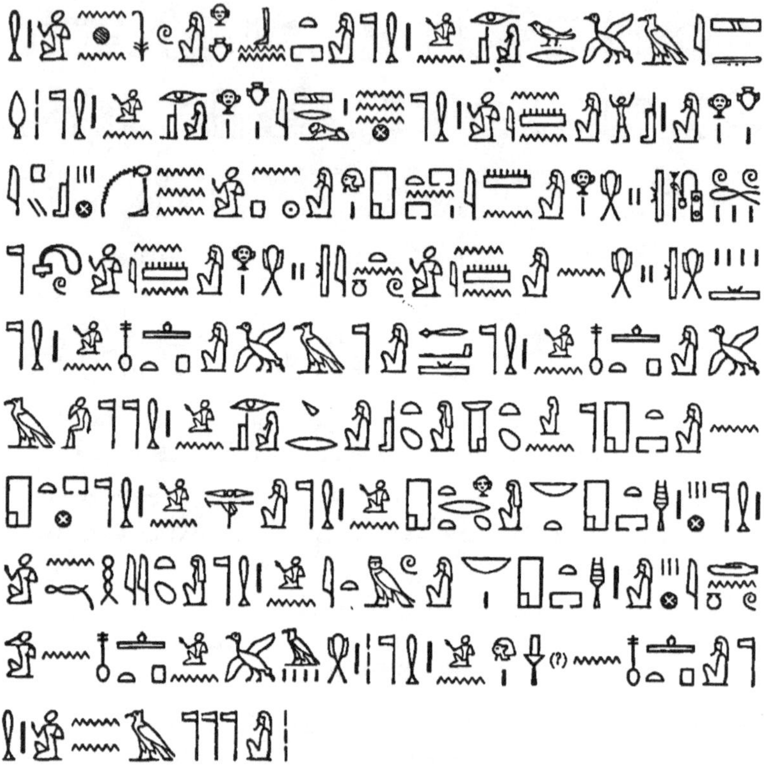

THE LAMENTATIONS OF ISIS AND NEPHTHYS.

III. 1.
2.
3.
4.
5.
6.
7.
8.
9.
10.
11.
12.
13.
IV. 1.
2.
3.
4.
5.

11.
12.
13.
14.
15.

THE LITANIES OF SEKER.

22.
23.
24.
25.
26.
27.
28.
29.
30.
31.
XIX. 1.
2.
3.
4.
5.
6.
7.
8.
9.
10.

11.
12.
13.
14.
15.
16.
17.
18.
19.
20.
21.
22.
23.
24.
25.
26.
27.
28.

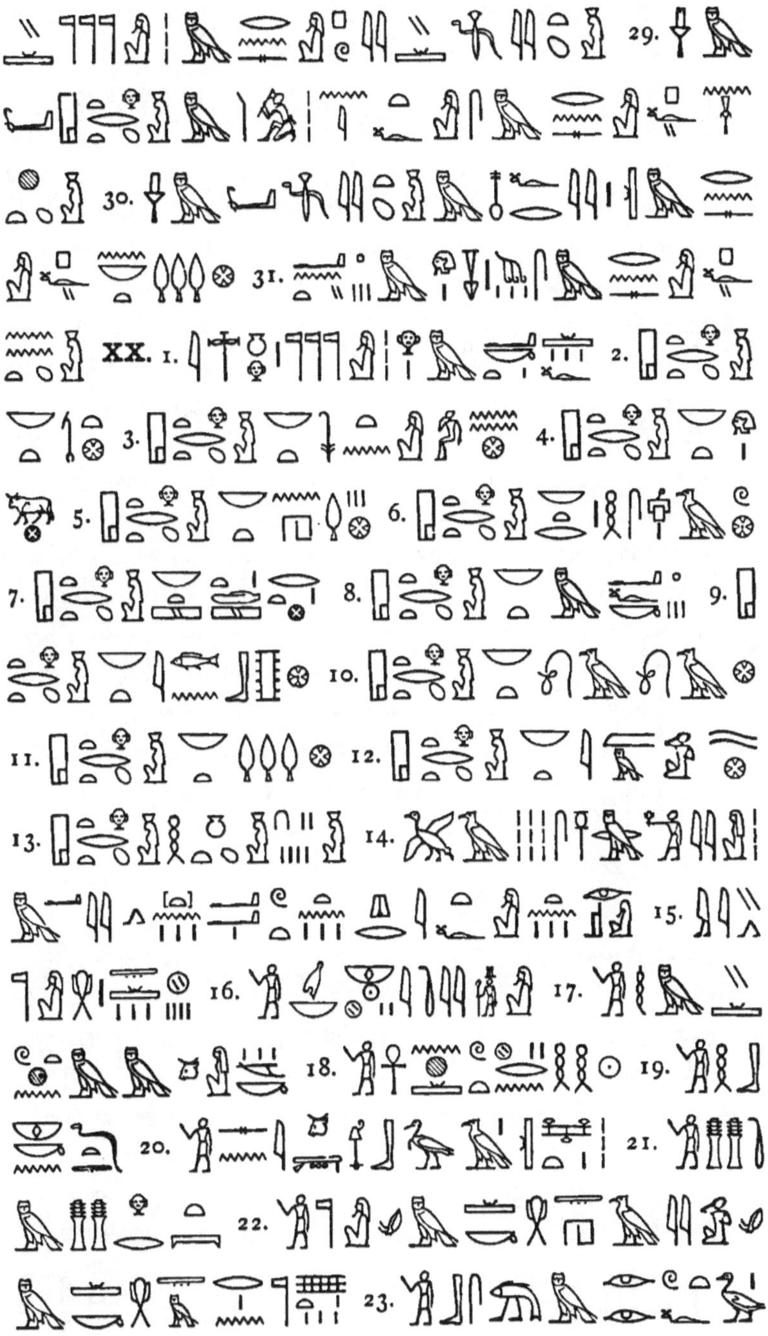

24.
25.
26.
27.
28.
29.
30.
31.
32.
XXI. 1.
2.
3.
4.
5.
6.

THE INSCRIPTION OF UNA.

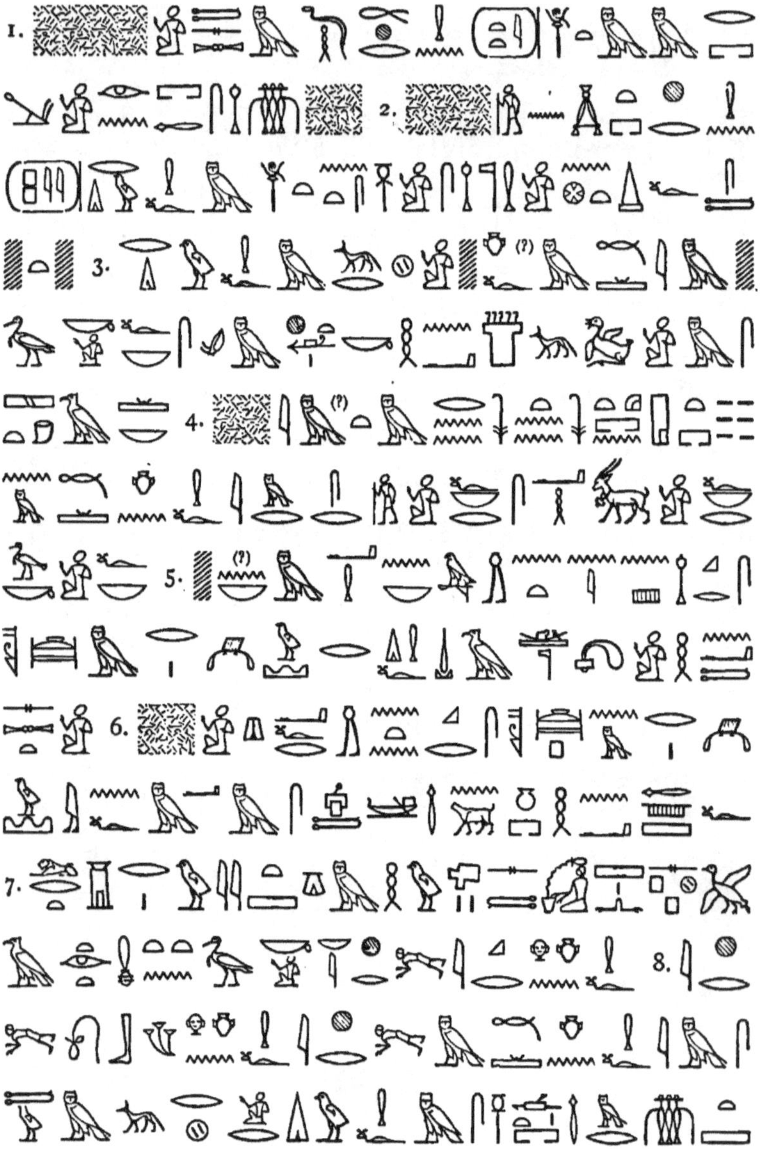

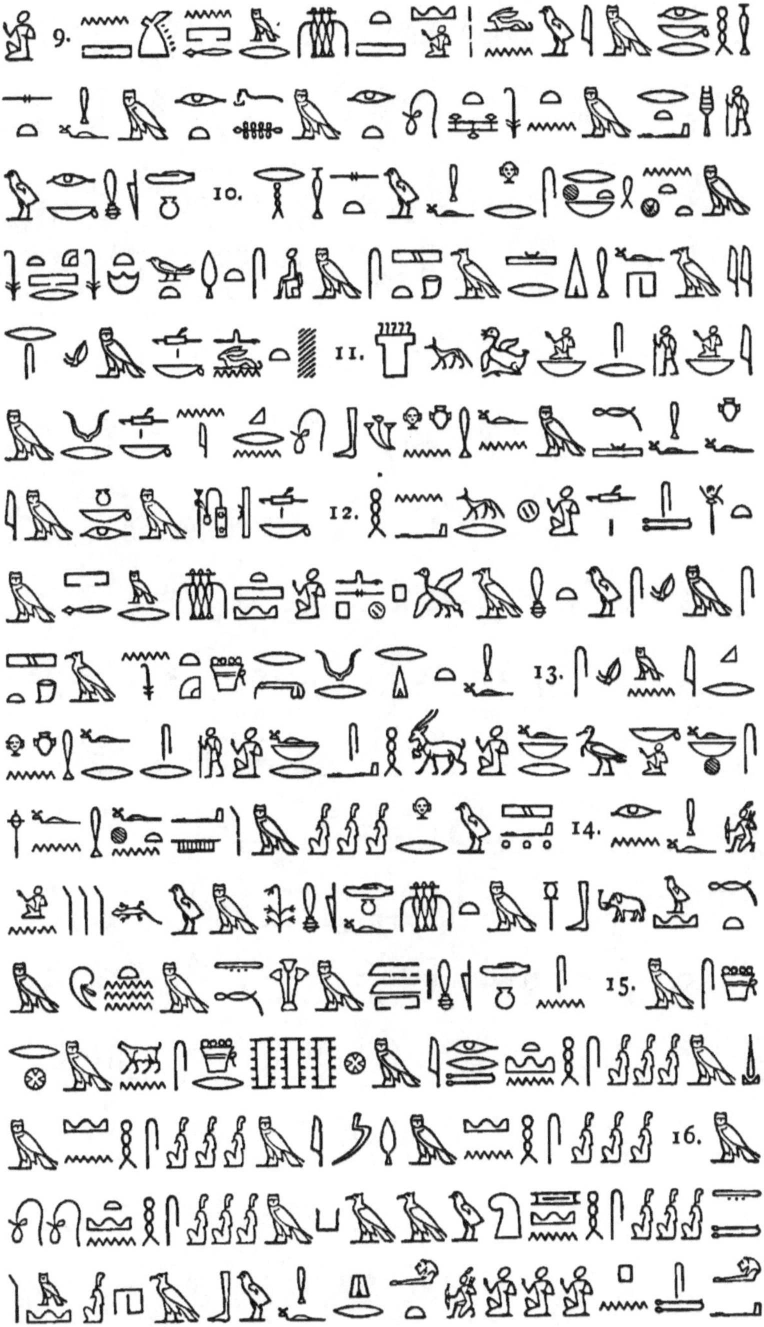
9.
10.
11.
12.
13.
14.
15.
16.

17.
18.
19.
20.
21.
22.
23.
24.
25.

26.
27.
28.
29.
30.
31.
32.
33.
34.

35.
36.
37.
38.
39.
40.
41.
42.
43.

THE INSCRIPTION OF CHNEMU-ḤETEP.

C.

E.
D.

F.

G.
H.

I.
J.

INSCRIPTIONS ON THE BASE OF THE OBELISK OF ḤĀTSHEPSU.

7.
8.
B. 1.
2.
3.
4.
5.
6.

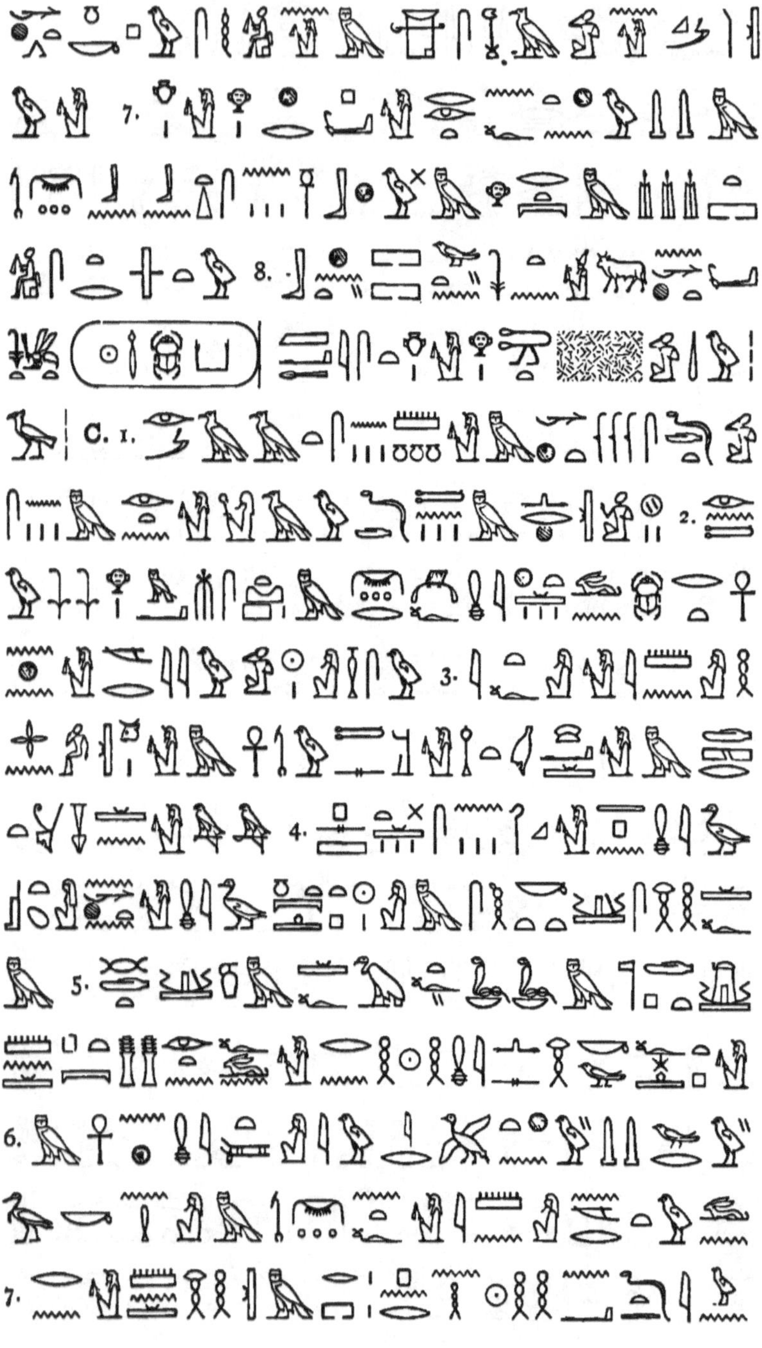

8.
D. 1.
2.
3.
4.
5.
6.
7.
8.

STELÆ OF NEXT-ÀMSU.

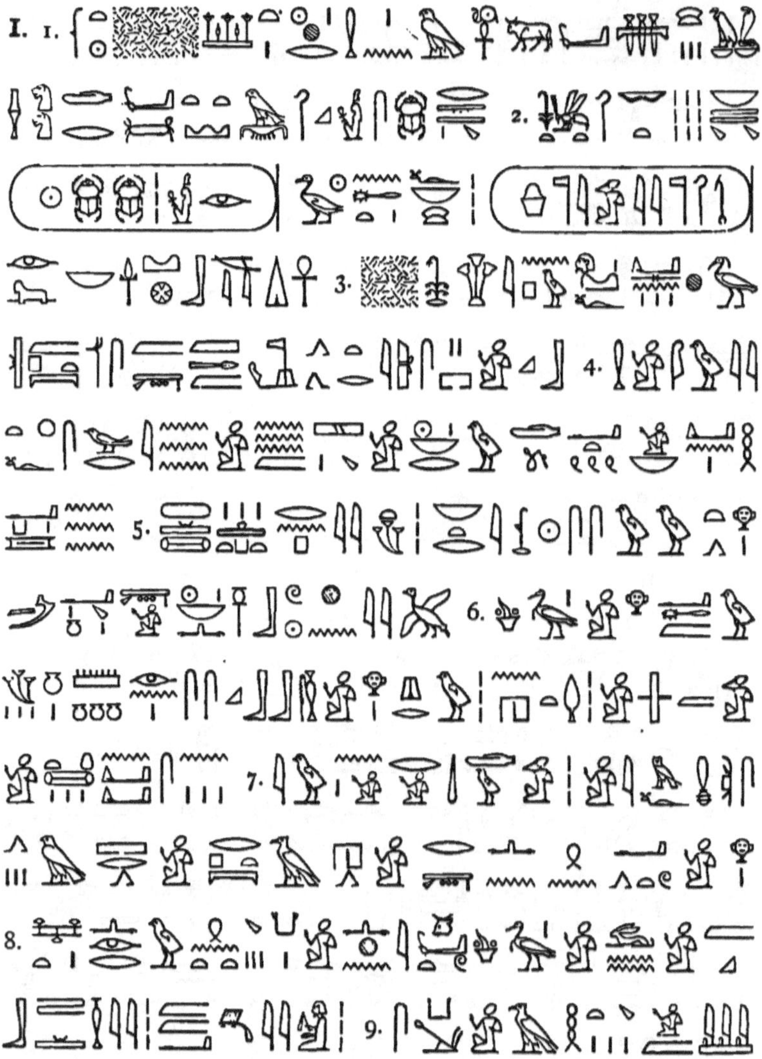

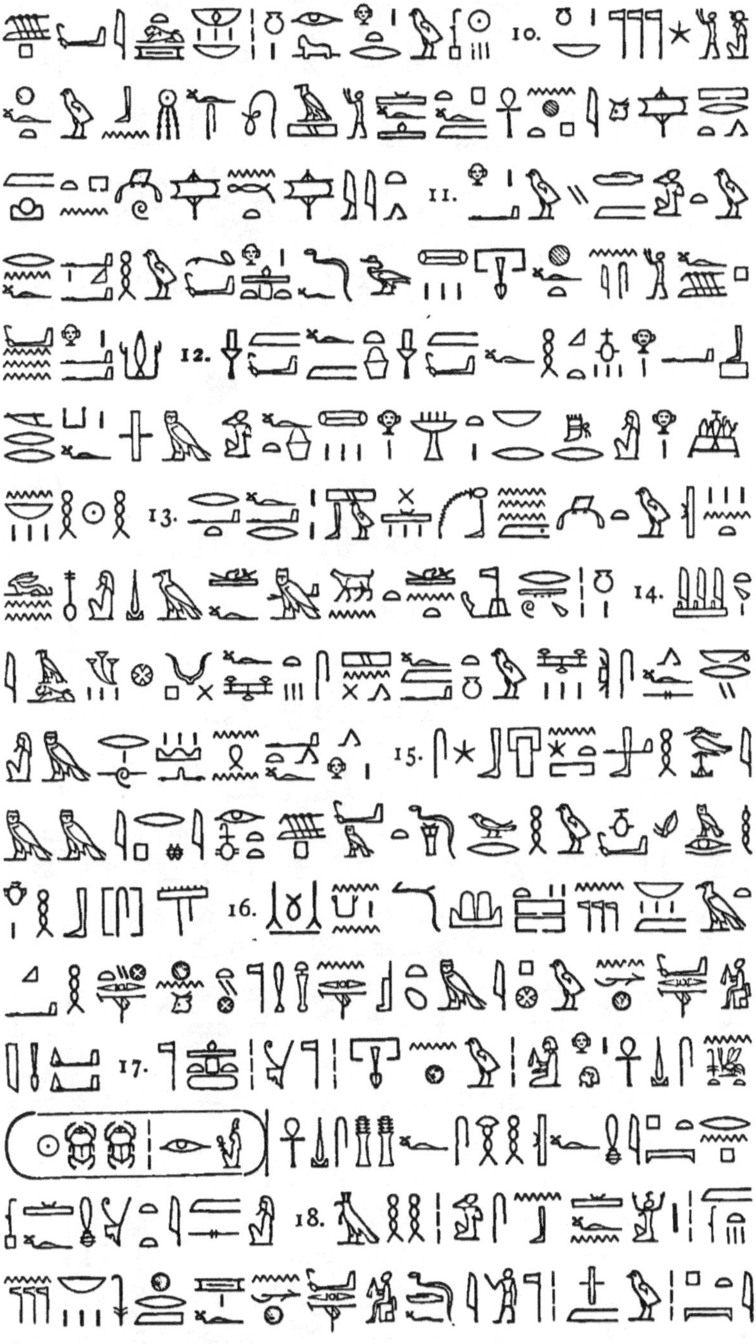
10.
11.
12.
13.
14.
15.
16.
17.
18.

THE BATTLE OF KADESH.

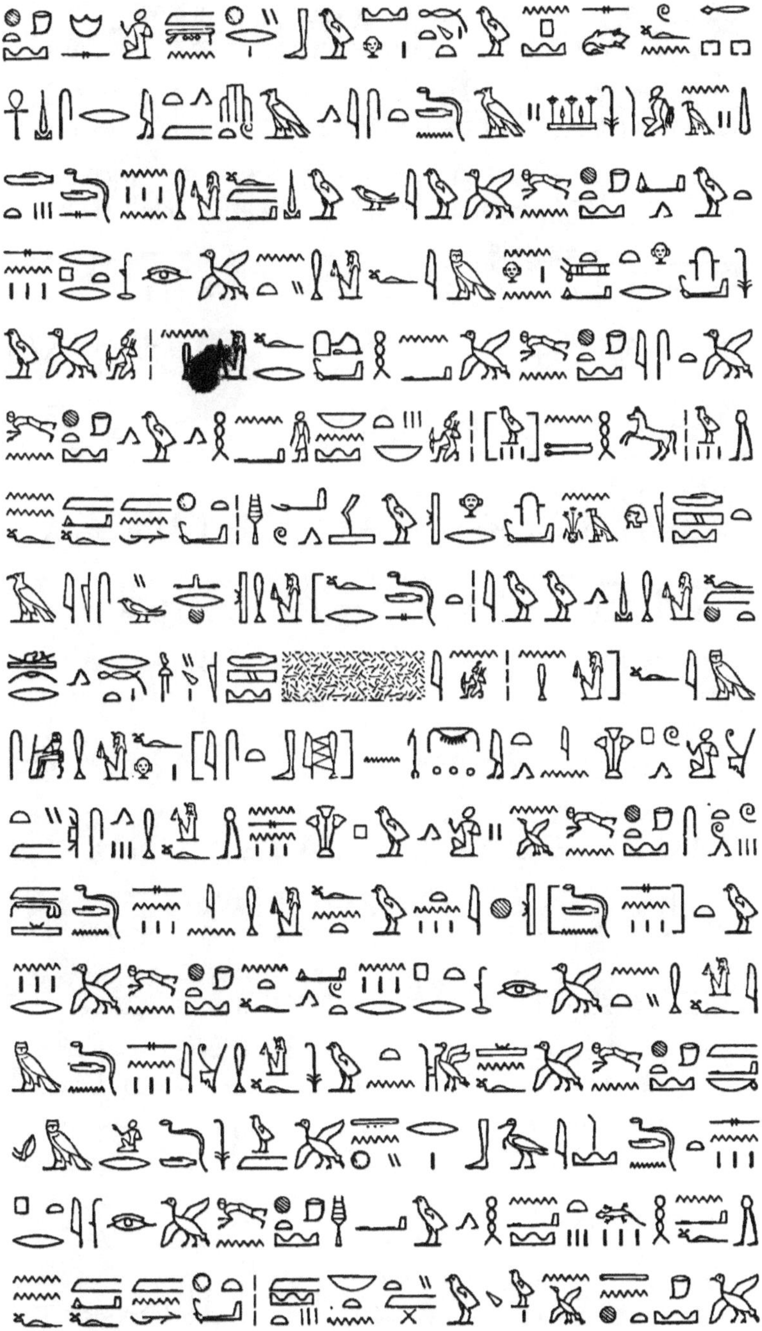

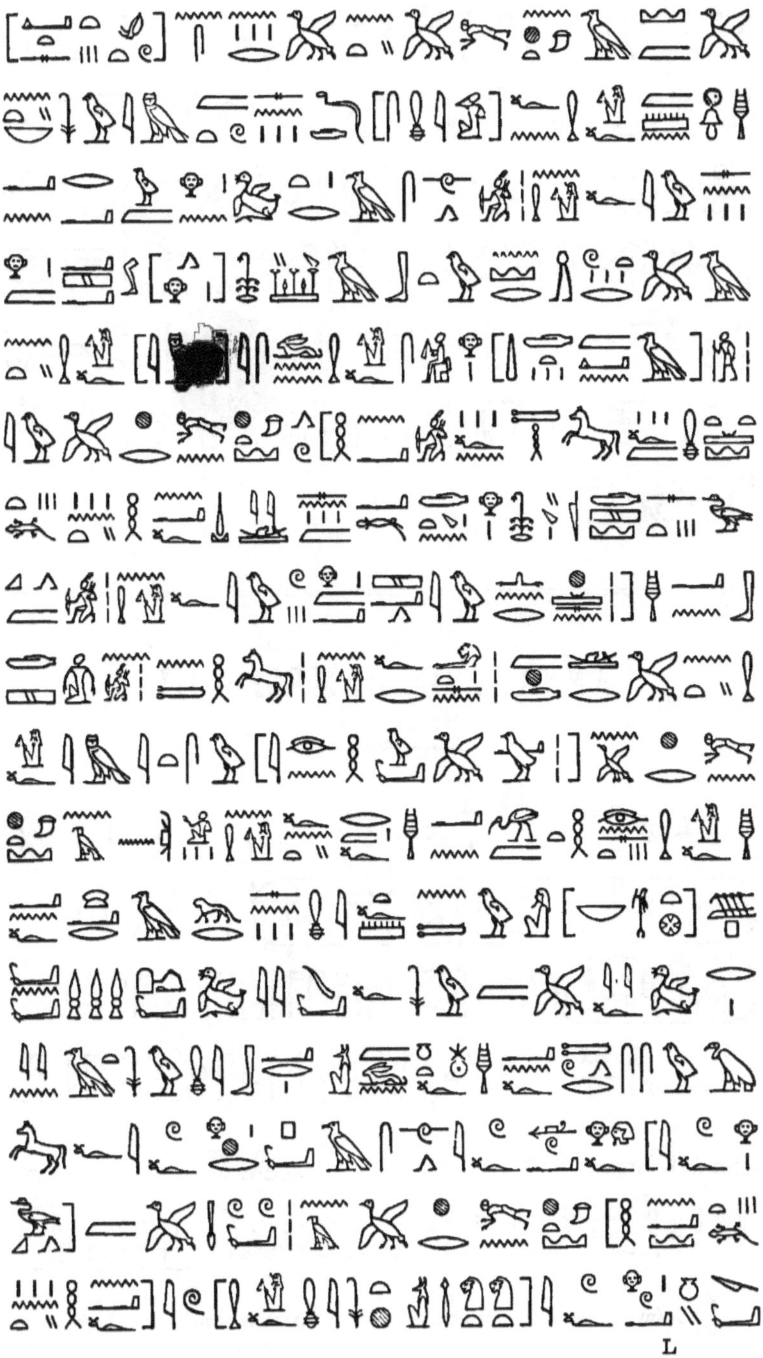

L

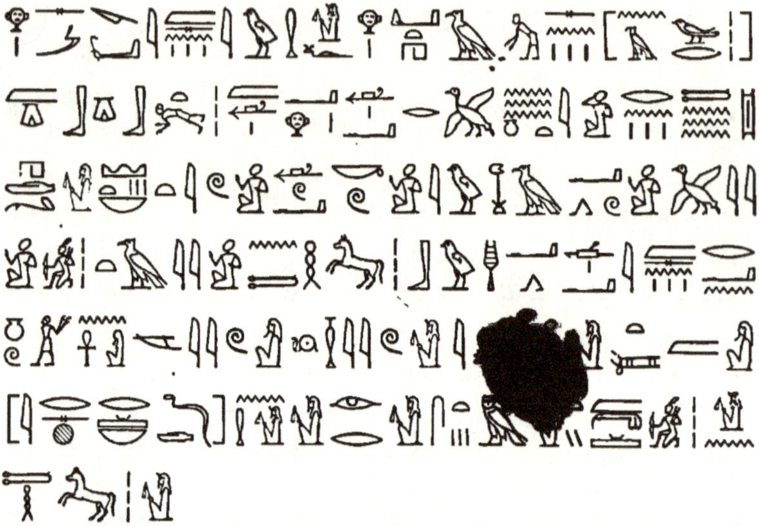

ANNALS OF RAMESES III.

* I am unable to transcribe the hieratic characters which occur here.

3.
4.
5.
6.
7.
8.

7.
8.
9.
10.
11.
IV. 1.

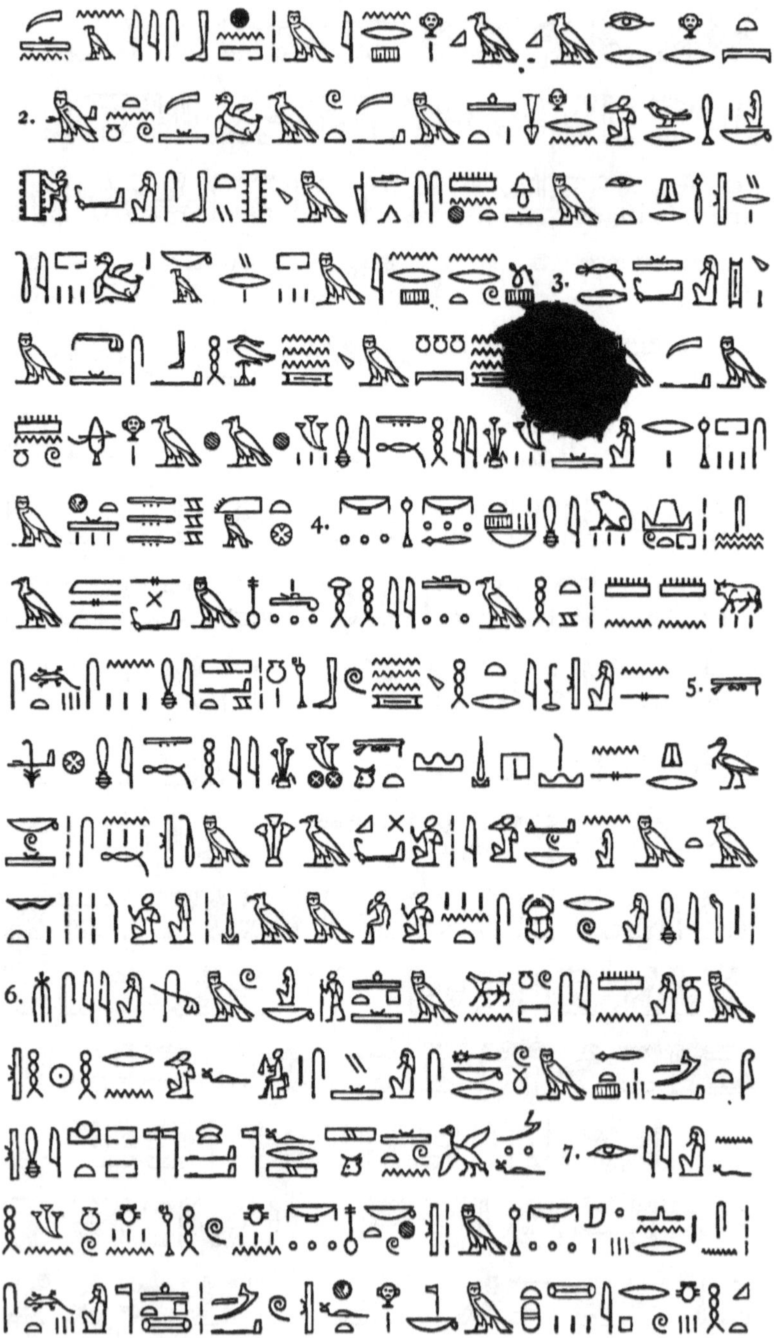
2.
3.
4.
5.
6.
7.

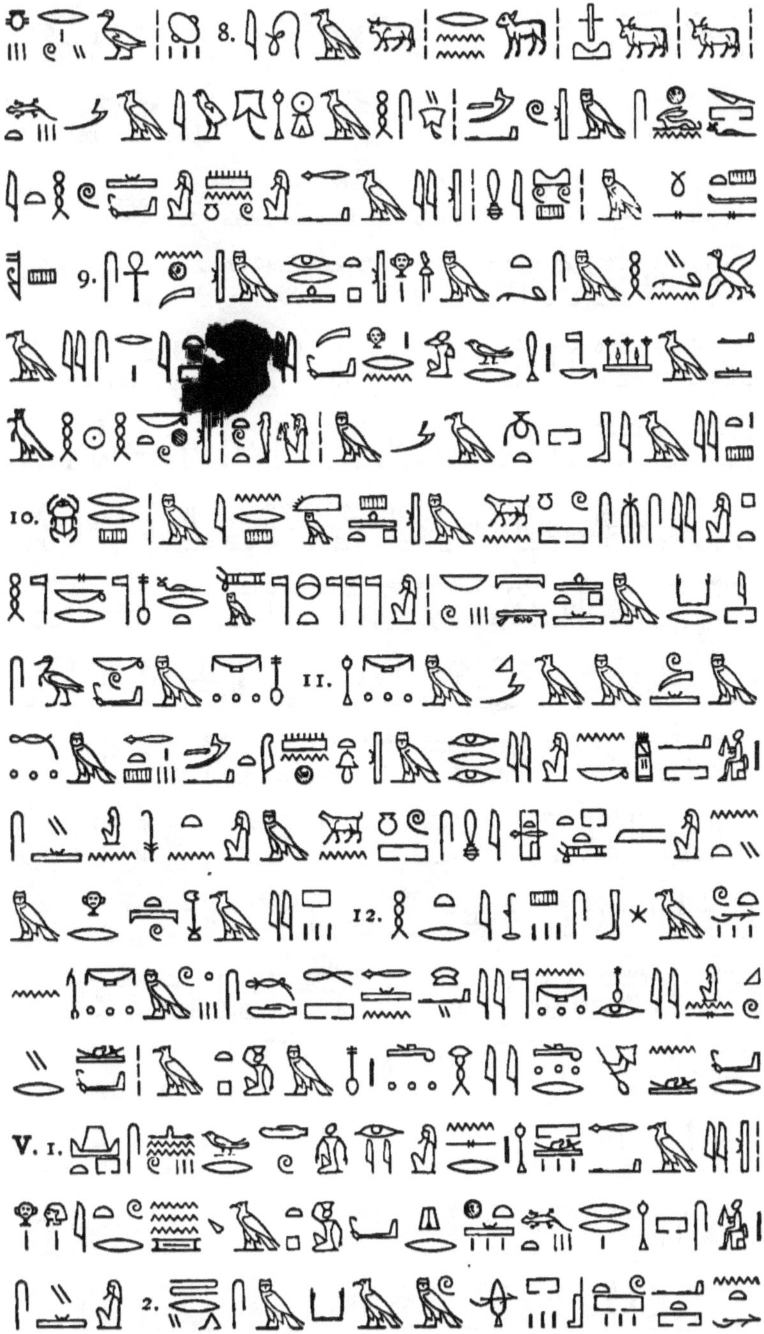

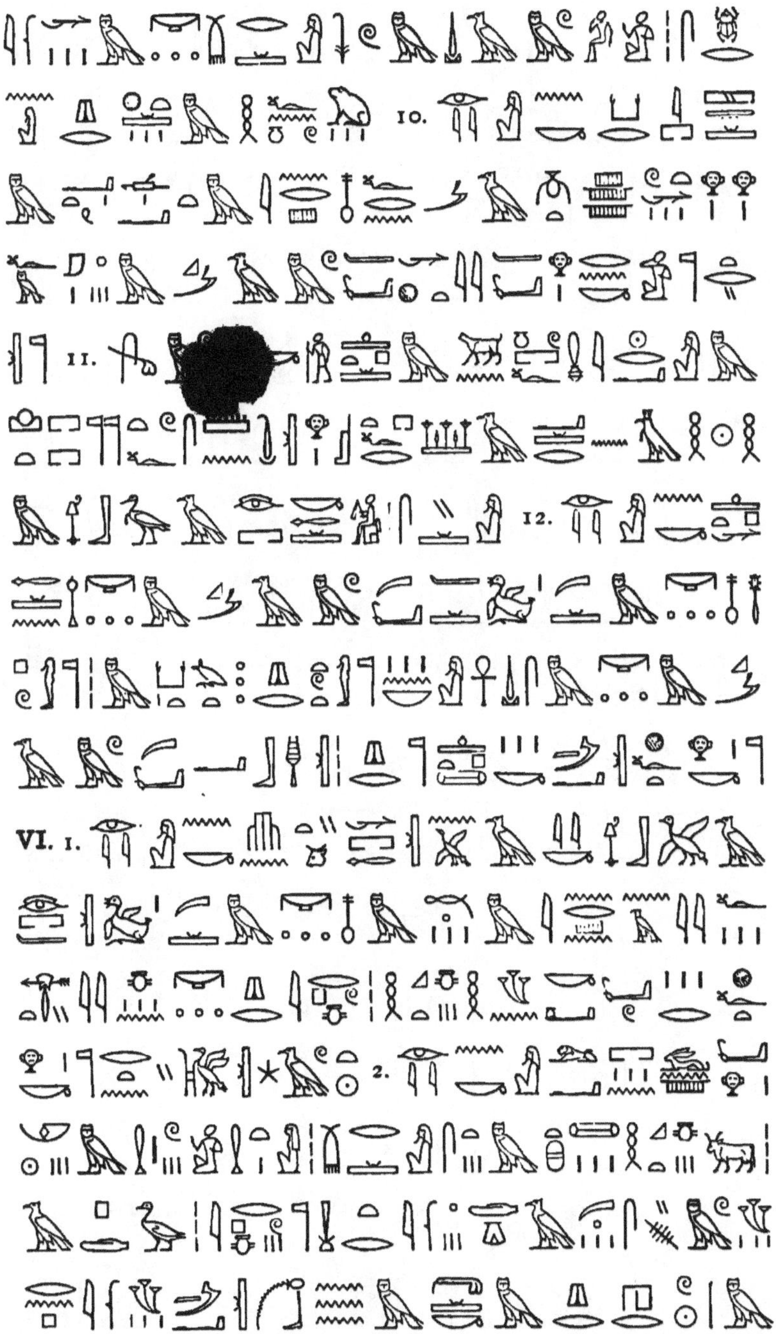
10.
11.
12.
VI. 1.
2.

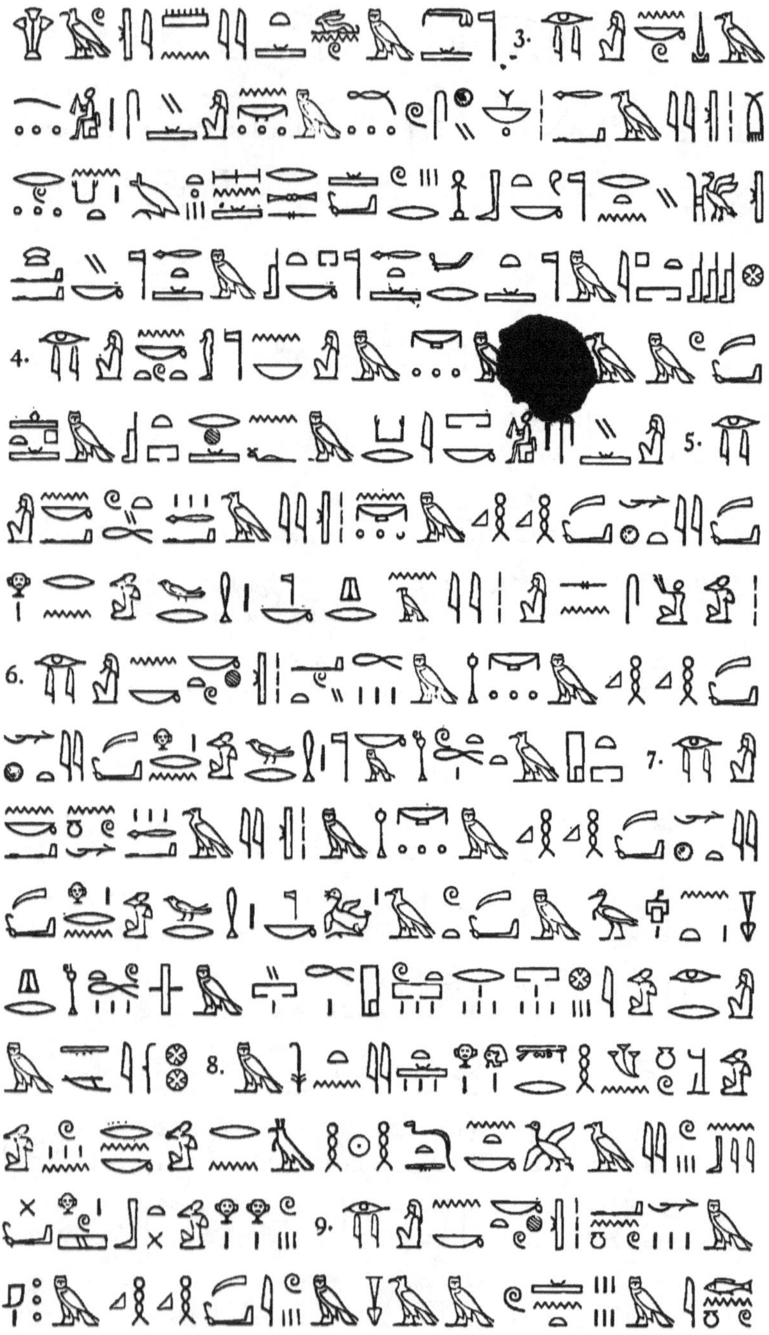

10.
11.
12.
13.
VII. 1.
(sic)
2.

* I am unable to transcribe the hieratic sign which occurs here.

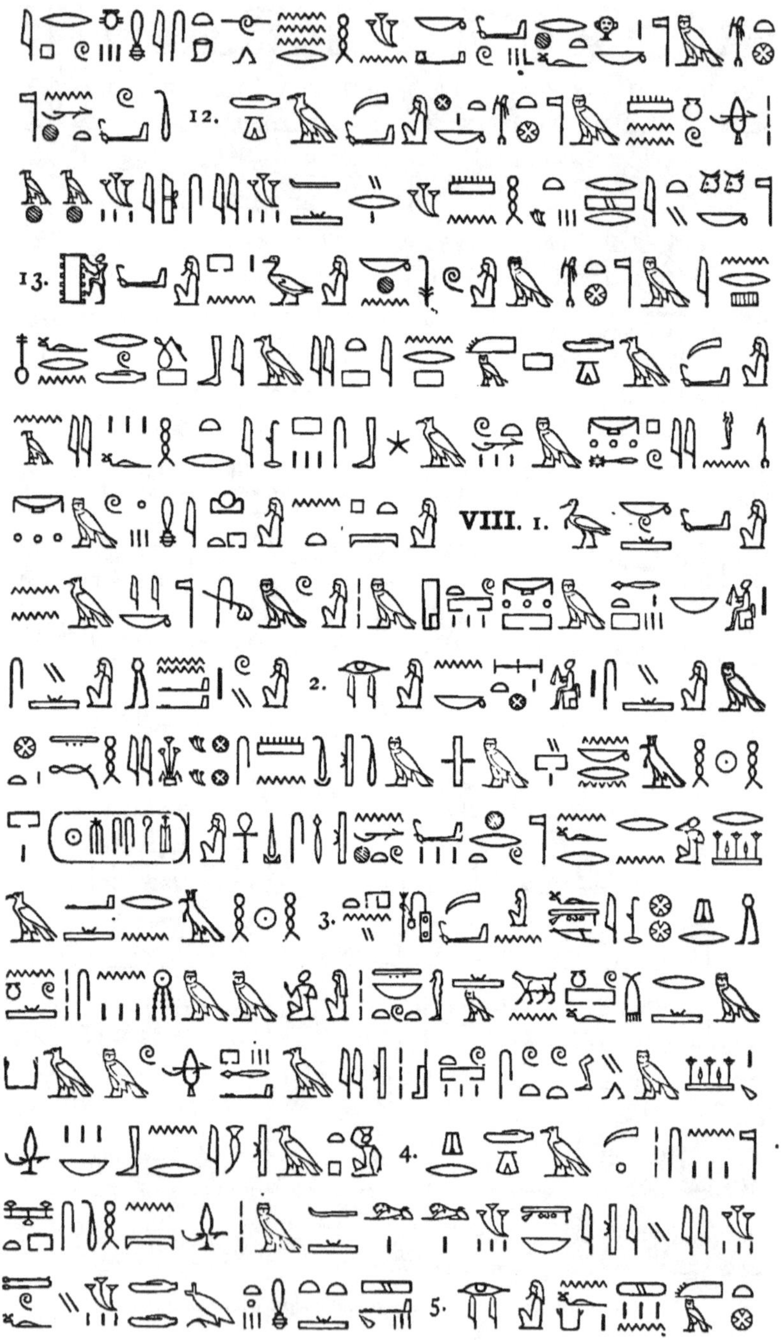
12.
13.
VIII. 1.
2.
3.
4.
5.

6.
7.
8.
9.
10.
11.

12.
13.
IX. 1.
2.
3.
4.

5.
6.
7.
8.
9.
XX. a. 1.
2.
3.
4.
5.
6.
7.
8.
9.
10.
11.
12.
13.
14.
15.
16.
17.

XX. *b.*

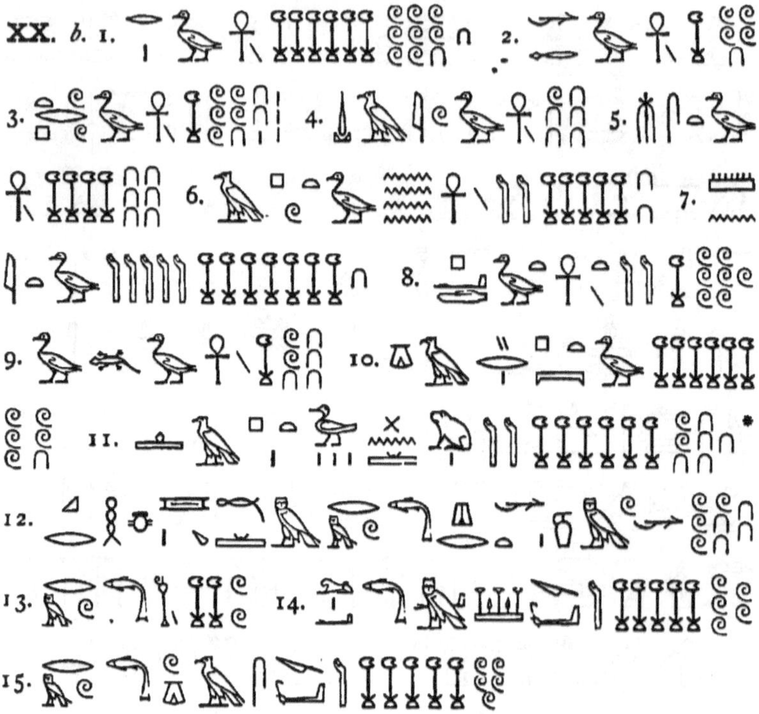

LXXV.

* The sum of the numbers of feathered fowl amounts to 126,254.

4.
5.
6.
7.
8.
9.

10.

LXXVI. 1.

2.

3.

4.

5.

6.
7.
8.
9.
10.

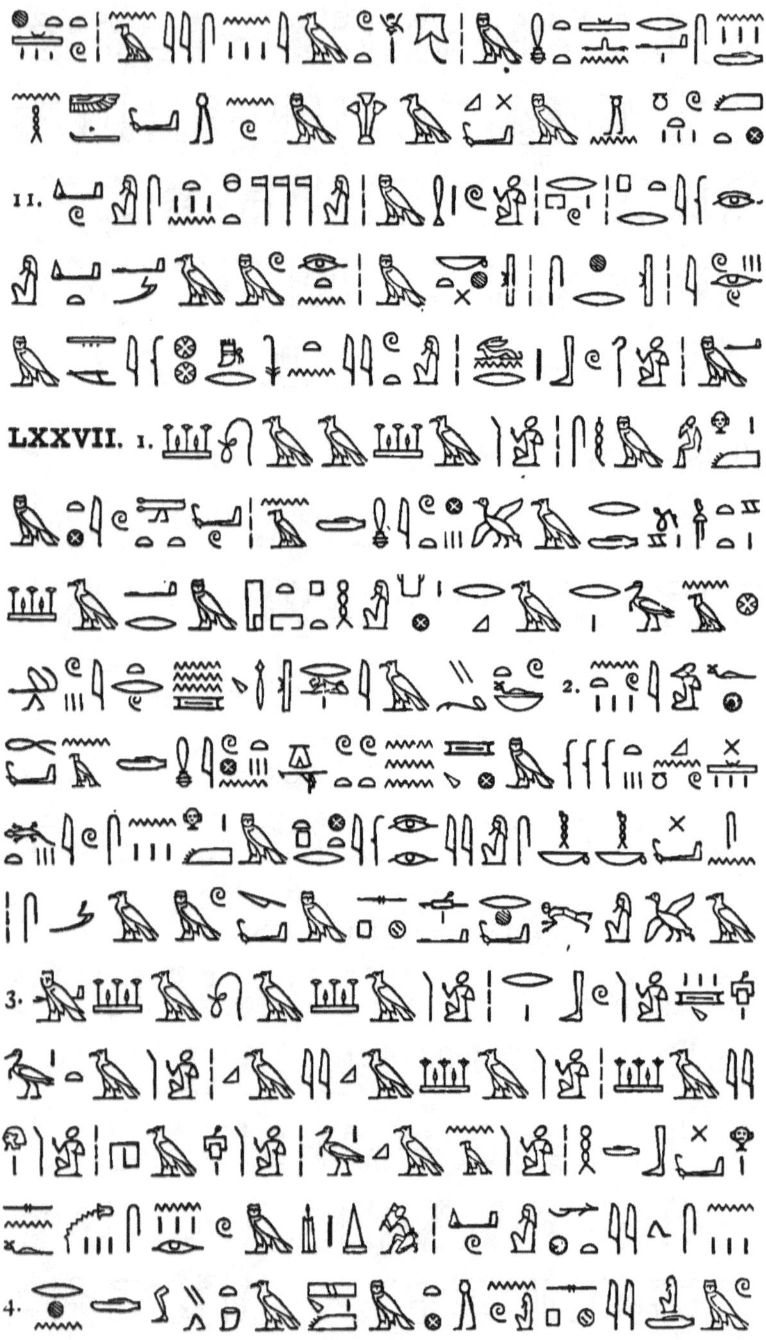
11.
LXXVII. 1.
2.
3.
4.

10.
11.
12.
13.
LXXVIII. 1.
2.

10.
11.
12.
13.
LXXIX. 1.
2.
3.

4.
5.
6.
7.
8.
9.

THE STELE OF PI-ĀNXI-MERI-ÀMEN.

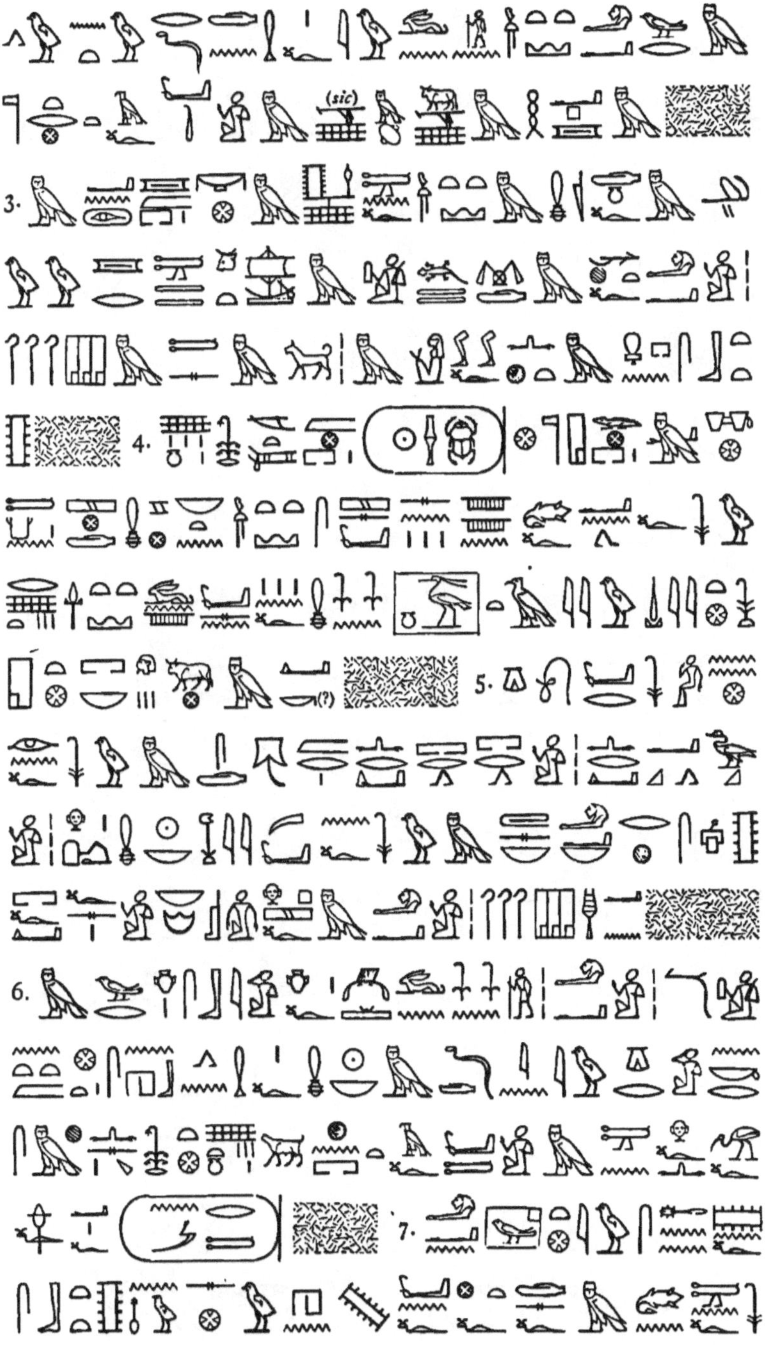

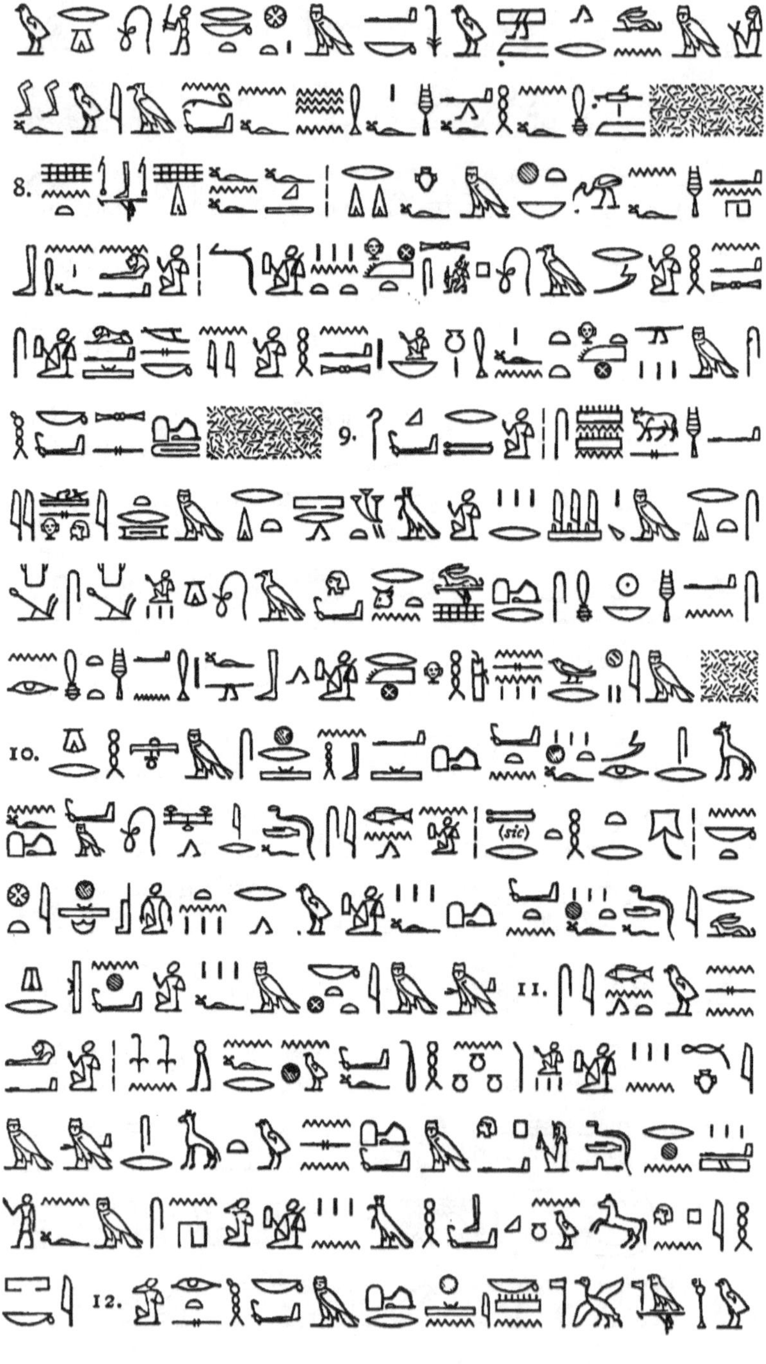
8.
9.
10.
(sic)
11.
12.

13.
14.
15.
16.
17.

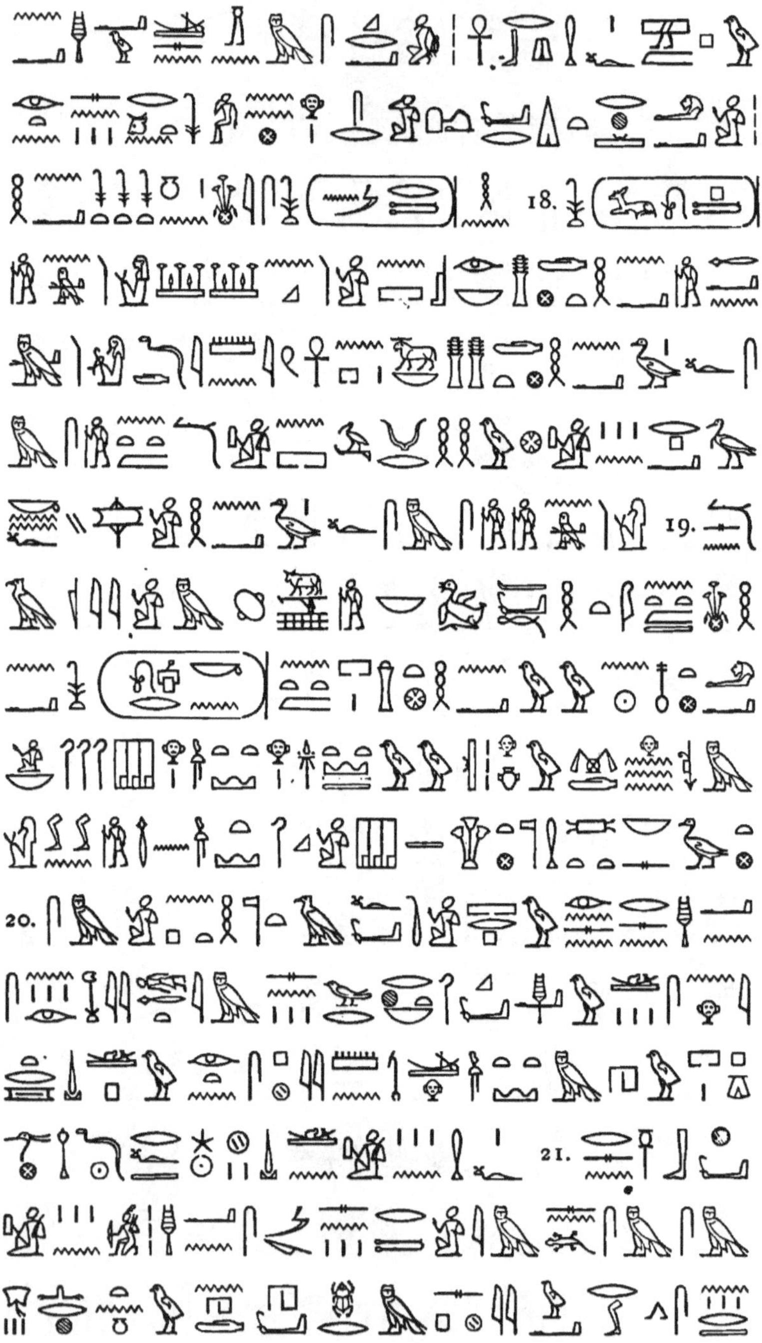
18.
19.
20.
21.

22.
23.
24.
25.
26.

27.
28.
29.
30.
31.

32.
33.
34.
(sic)
lacuna of 16 lines.
51.
52.
53.
(sic)

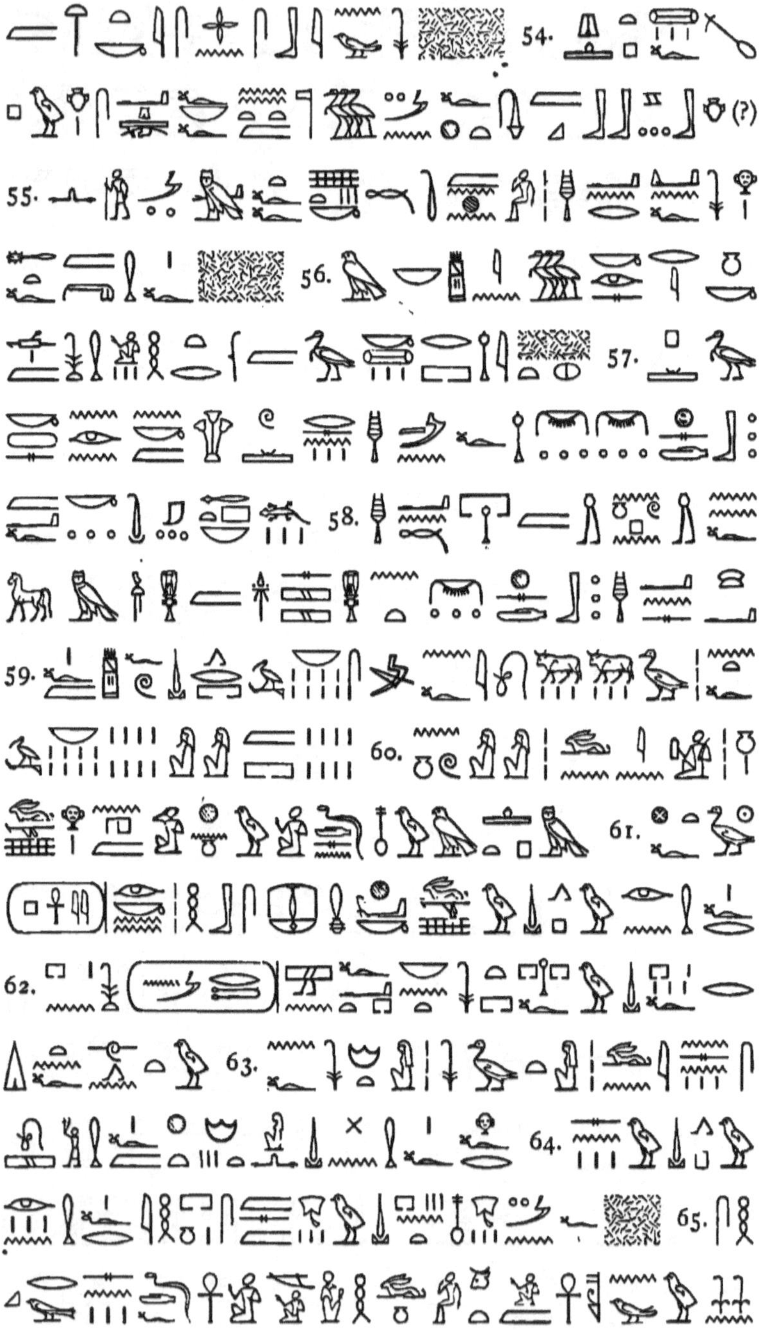
54.
55.
56.
57.
58.
59.
60.
61.
62.
63.
64.
65.

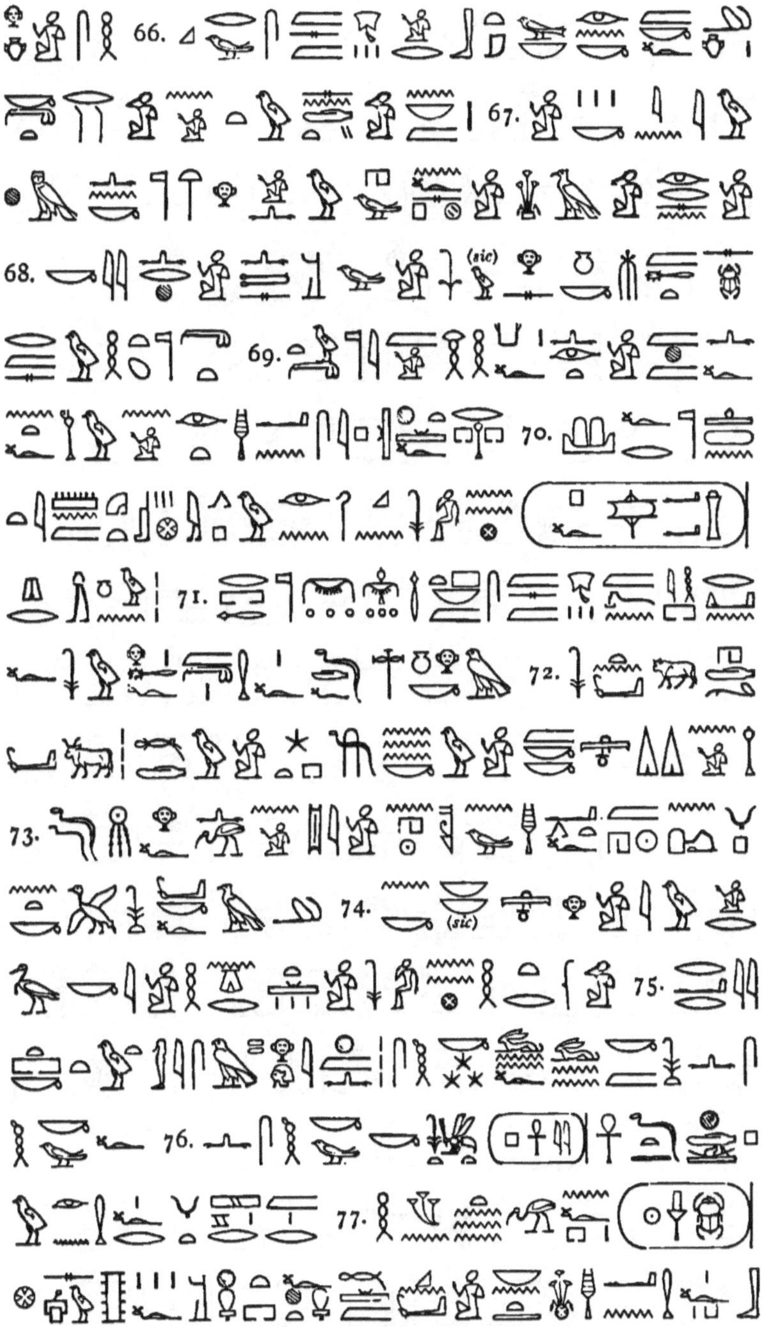

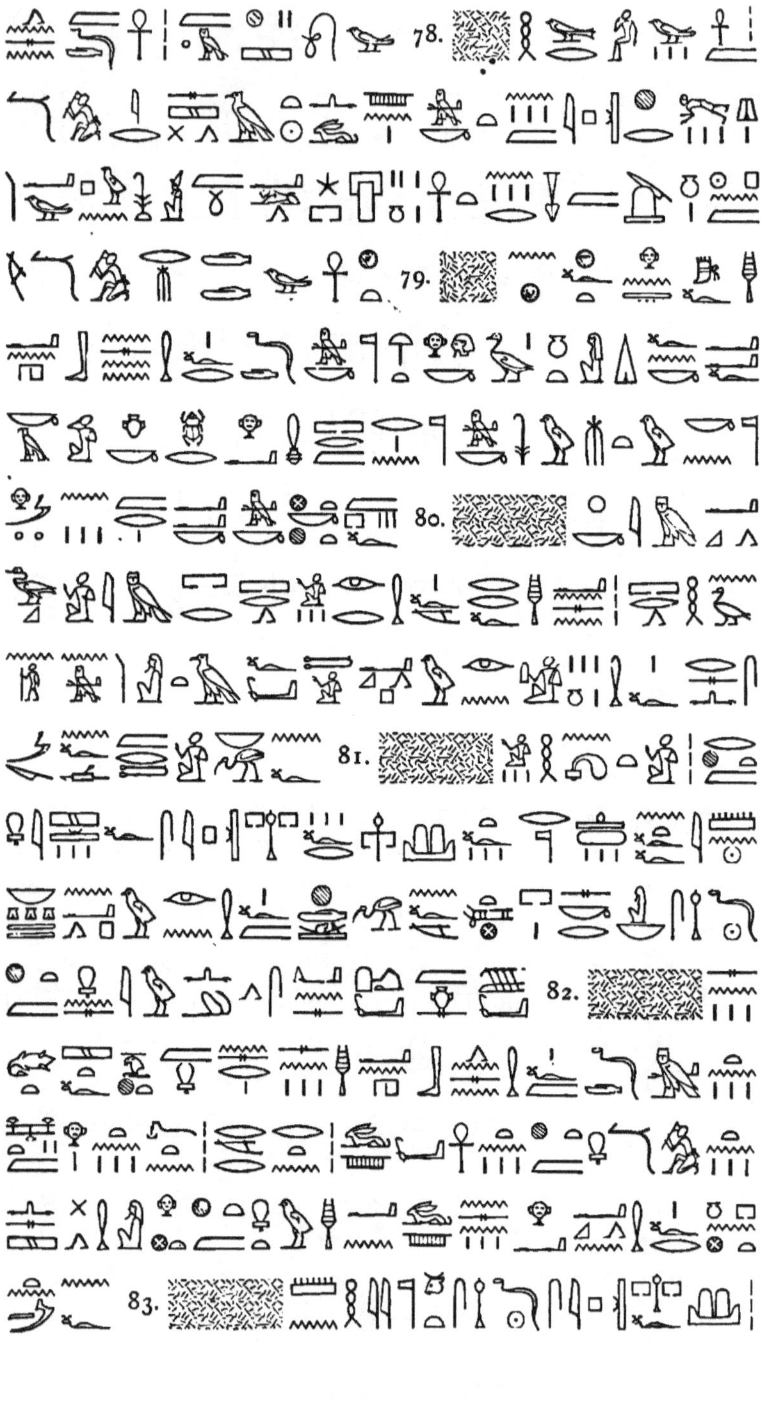
78.
79.
80.
81.
82.
83.

84.
85.
86.
87.

88.
89.
90.
91.
92.

Q

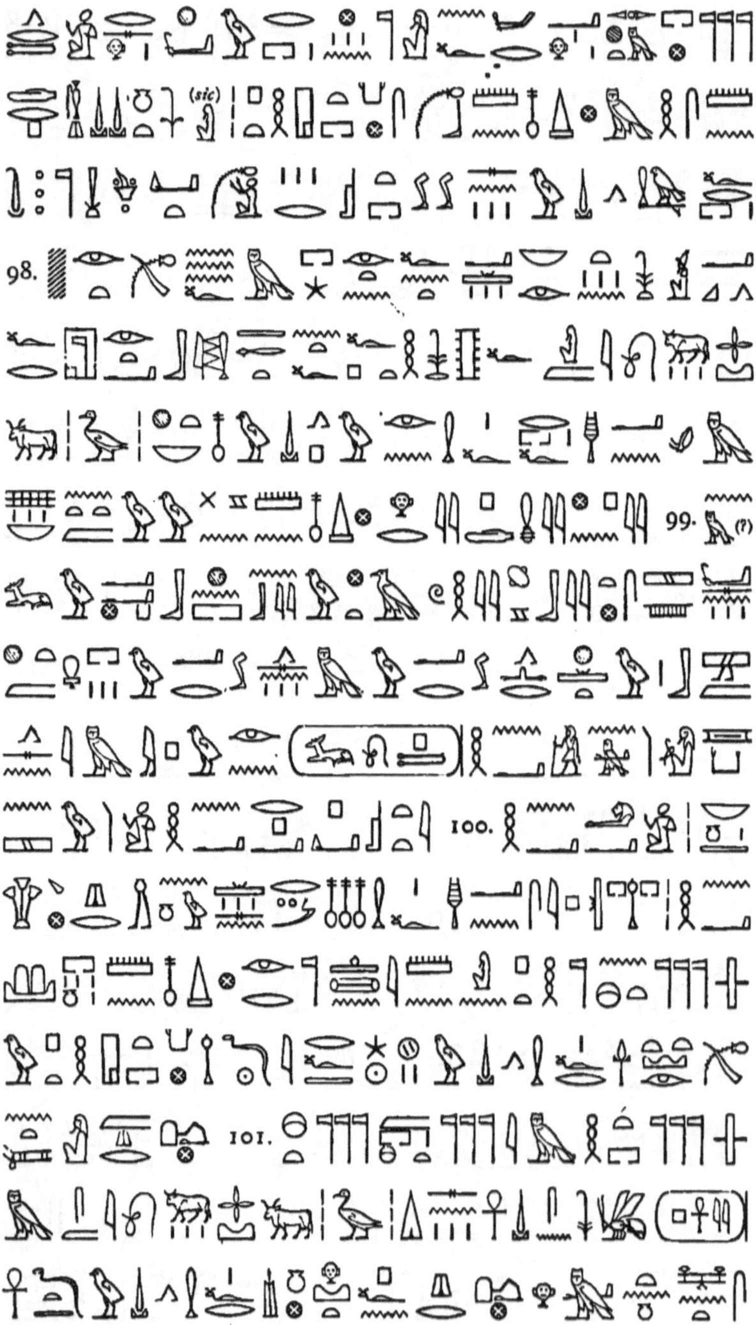
(sic)
98.
99.
(?)
100.
101.

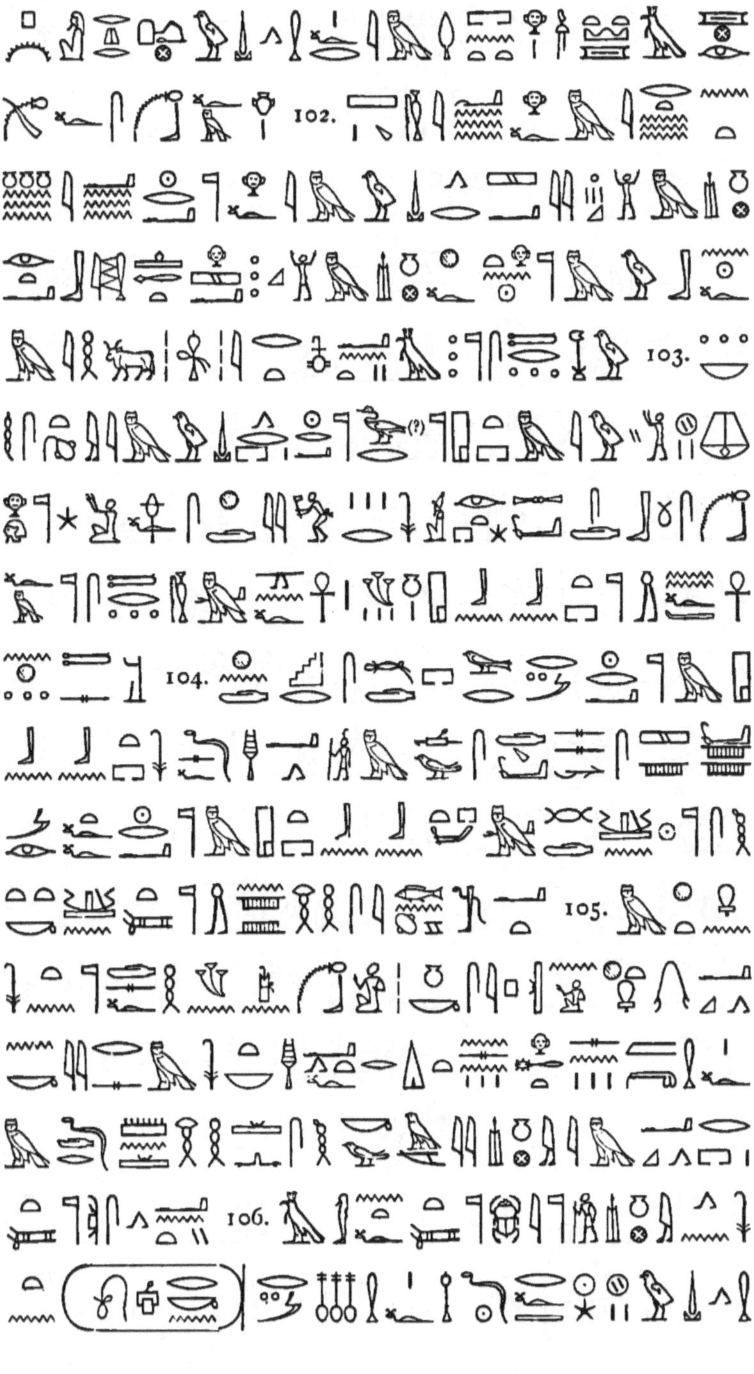
102.
103.
104.
105.
106.

107.
108.
109.
110.
111.

112.
113.
114.
115.

116.
117.
118.
119.
2 inches broken.
120.
3 inch broken.
121.
2 inches broken.
122.
123.
124.
125.
126.

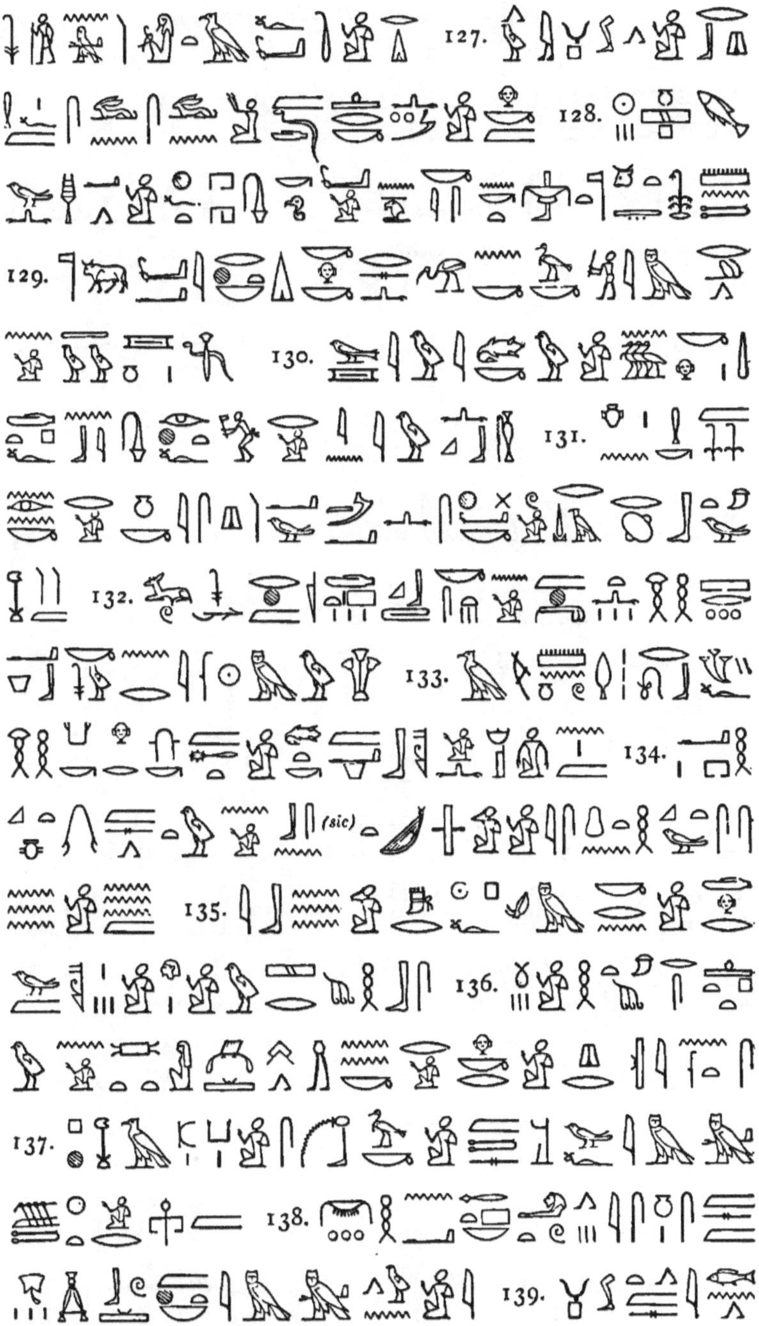
127.
128.
129.
130.
131.
132.
133.
134.
(sic)
135.
136.
137.
138.
139.

140.
141.
142.
143.
144.
145.
146.
147.
148.
149.
150.
151.
152.
153.

THE DECREE OF CANOPUS.

R

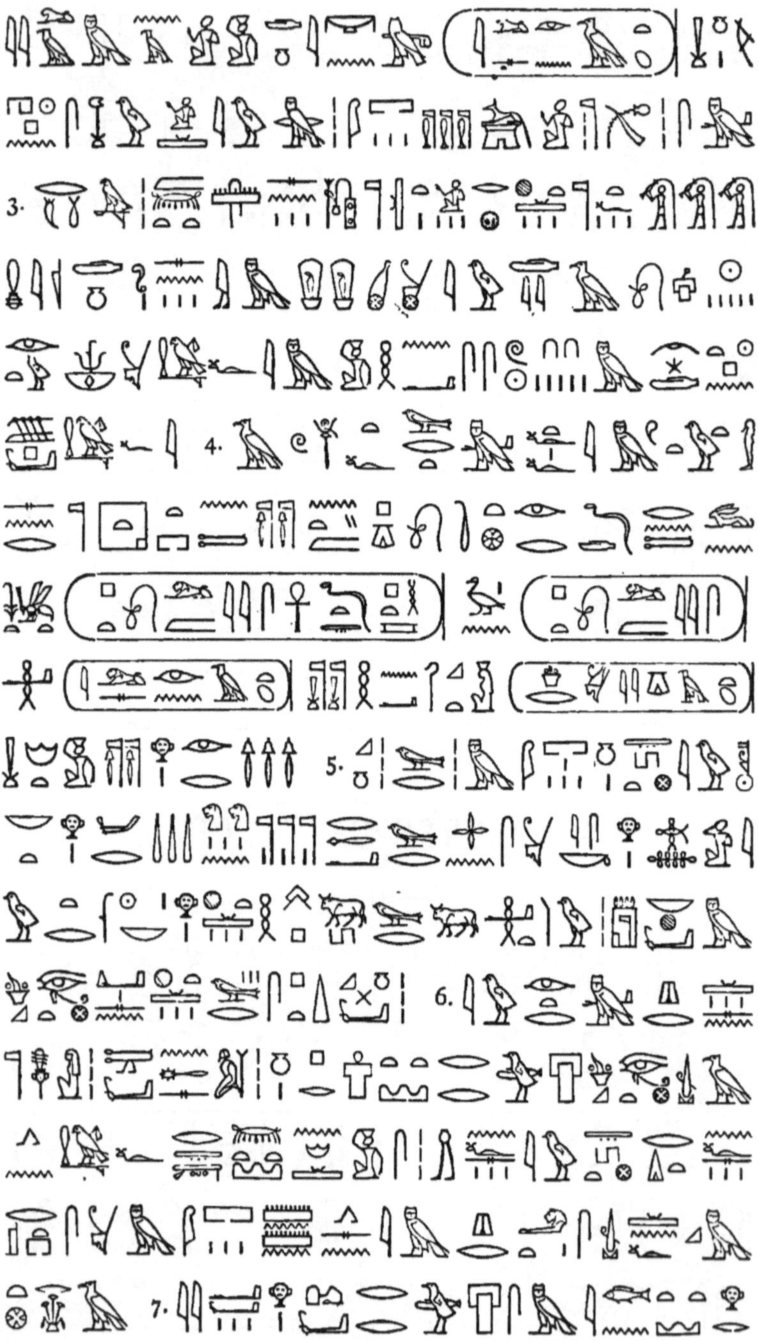

8.
9.
10.
11.

12.
13.
14.
15.

21.
22.
23.
24.

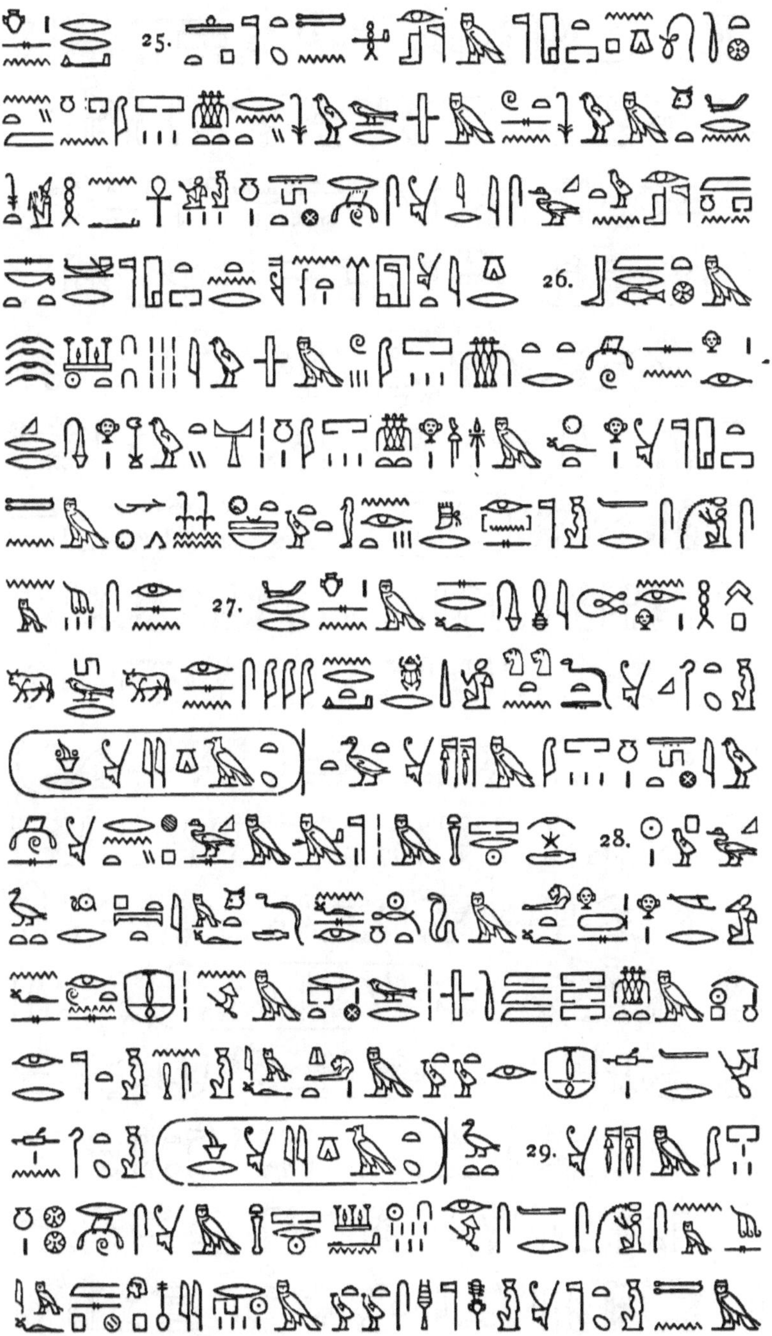
25.
26.
27.
28.
29.

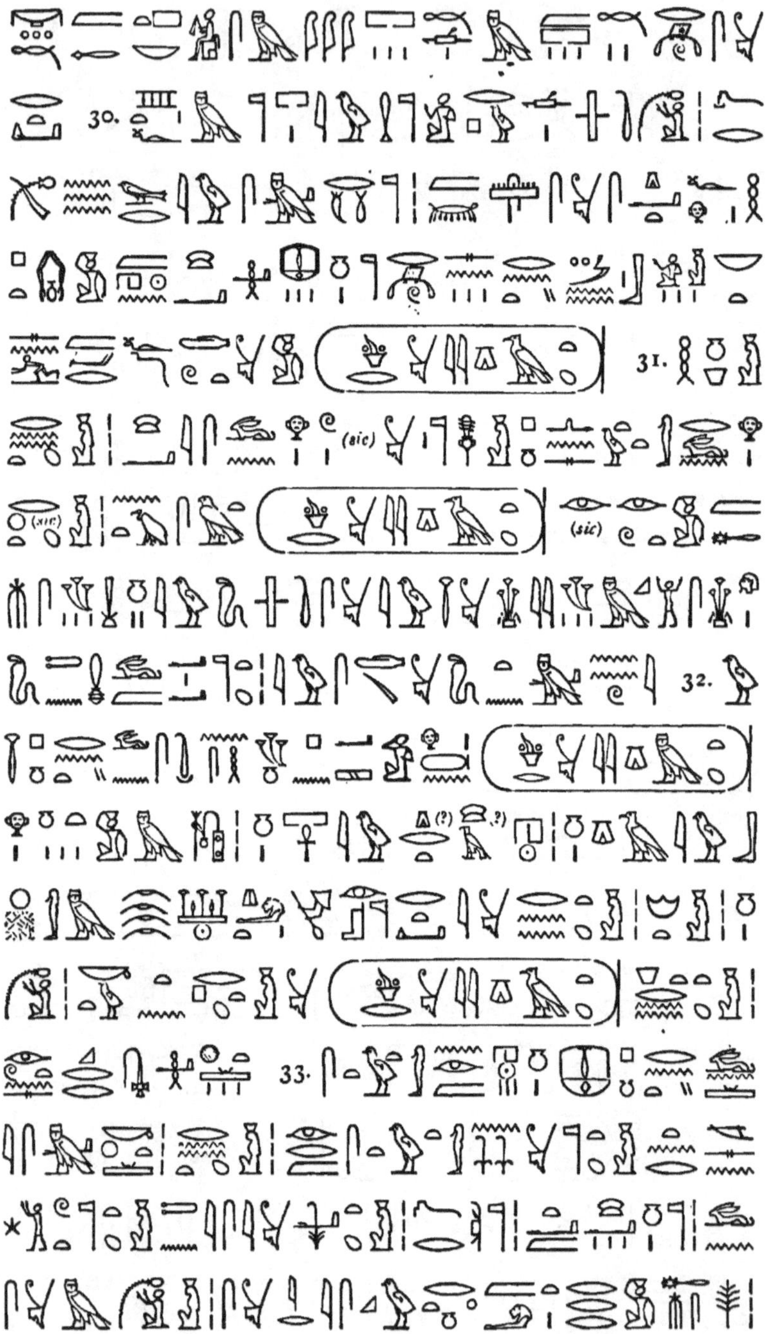
30.
31.
(sic)
(sic)
(sic)
32.
(?)
(?)
33.

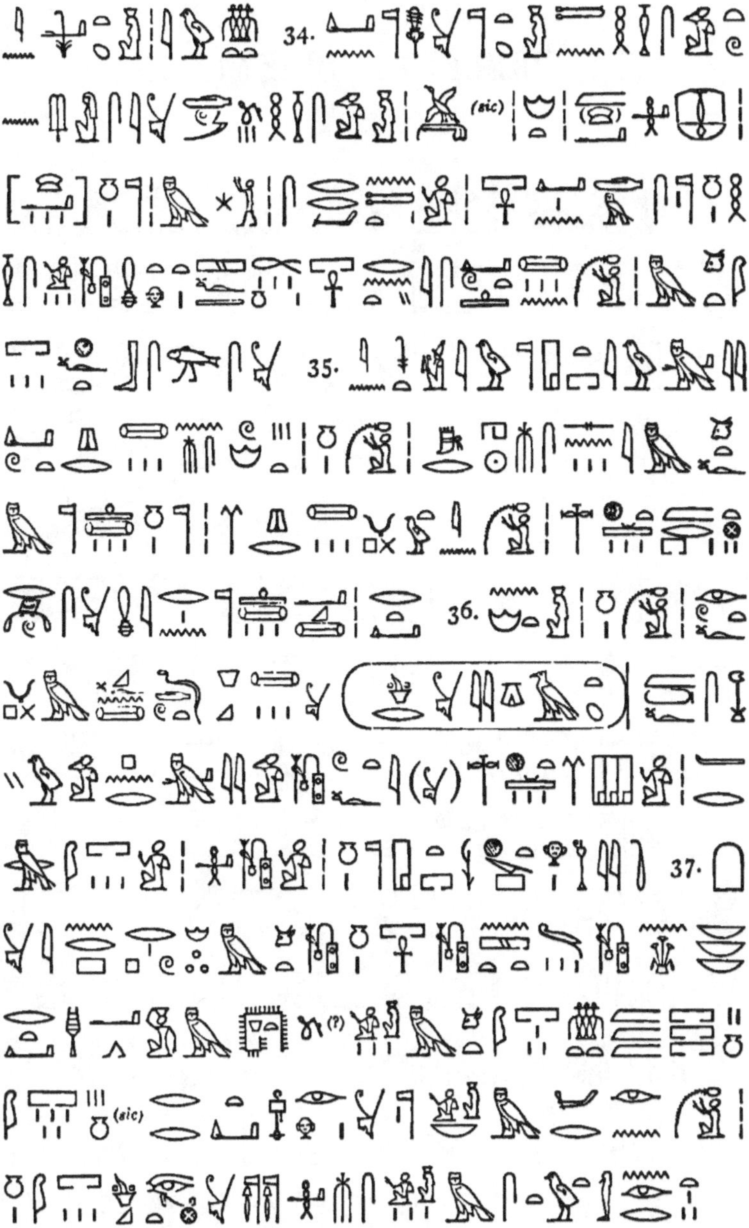
34.
(sic)
35.
36.
37.
(?)
(sic)

THE PRECEPTS OF KAKEMNA.

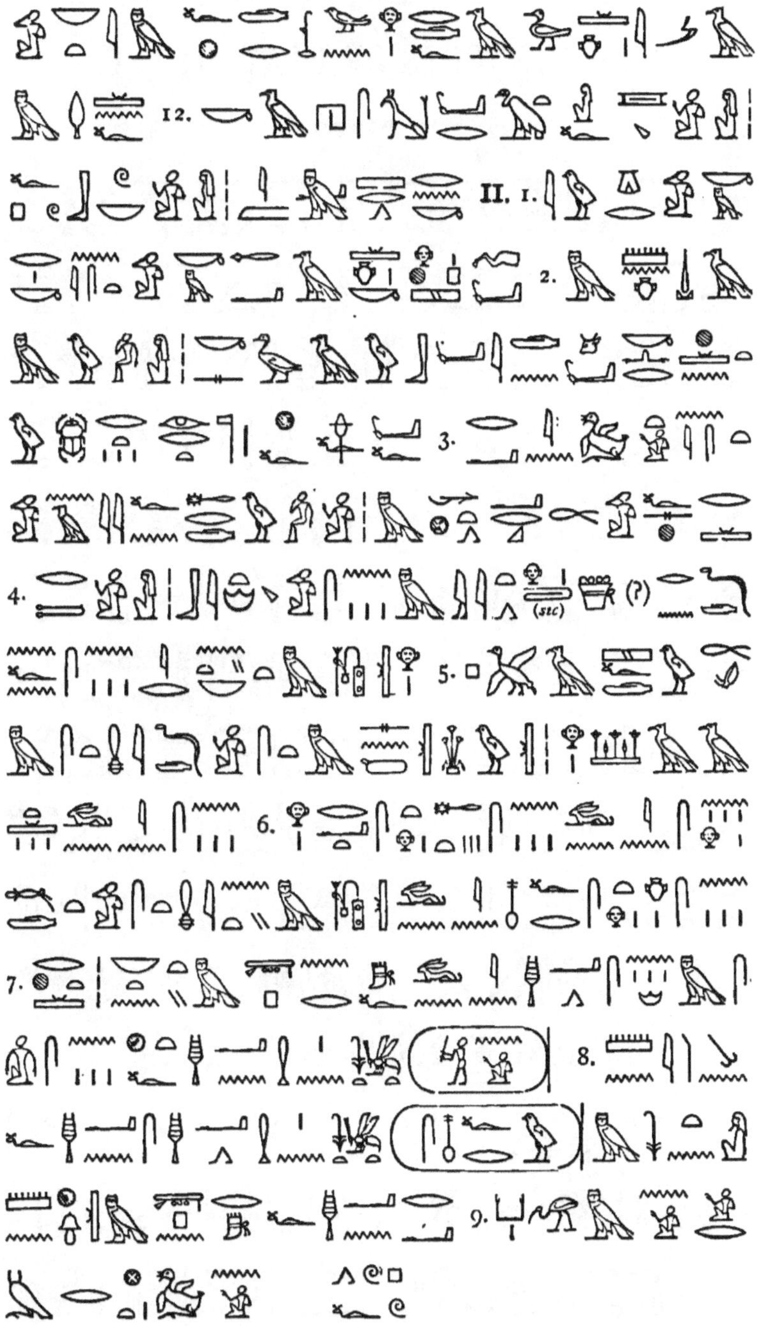
12.
II. 1.
2.
3.
4.
(sic)
(?)
5.
6.
7.
8.
9.

THE PRECEPTS OF PTAḤ-ḤETEP.

6.
7.
8.
9.
10.
11.
12.
13.
14.

VI. 1.
2.
3.
4.
5.
6.
7.
8.
9.

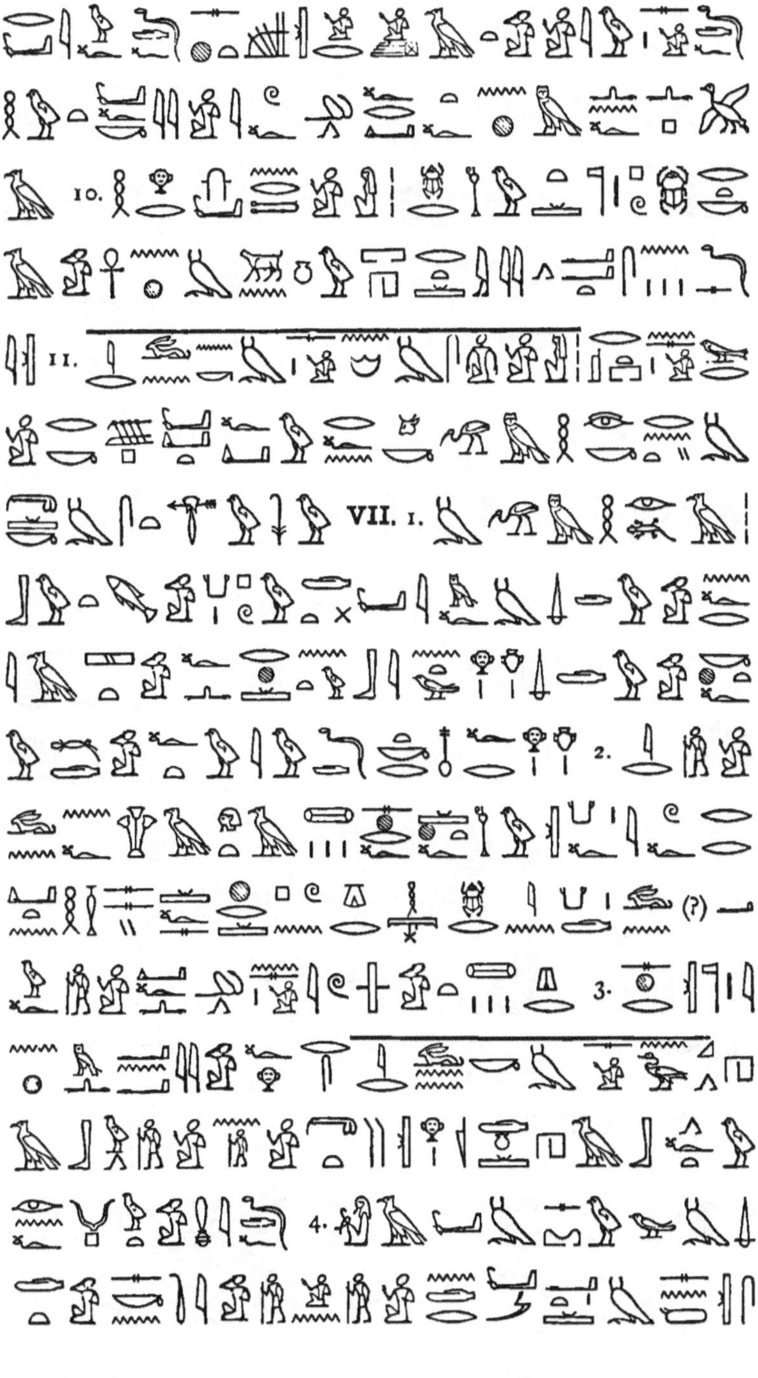
10.
11.
VII. 1.
2.
(?)
3.
4.

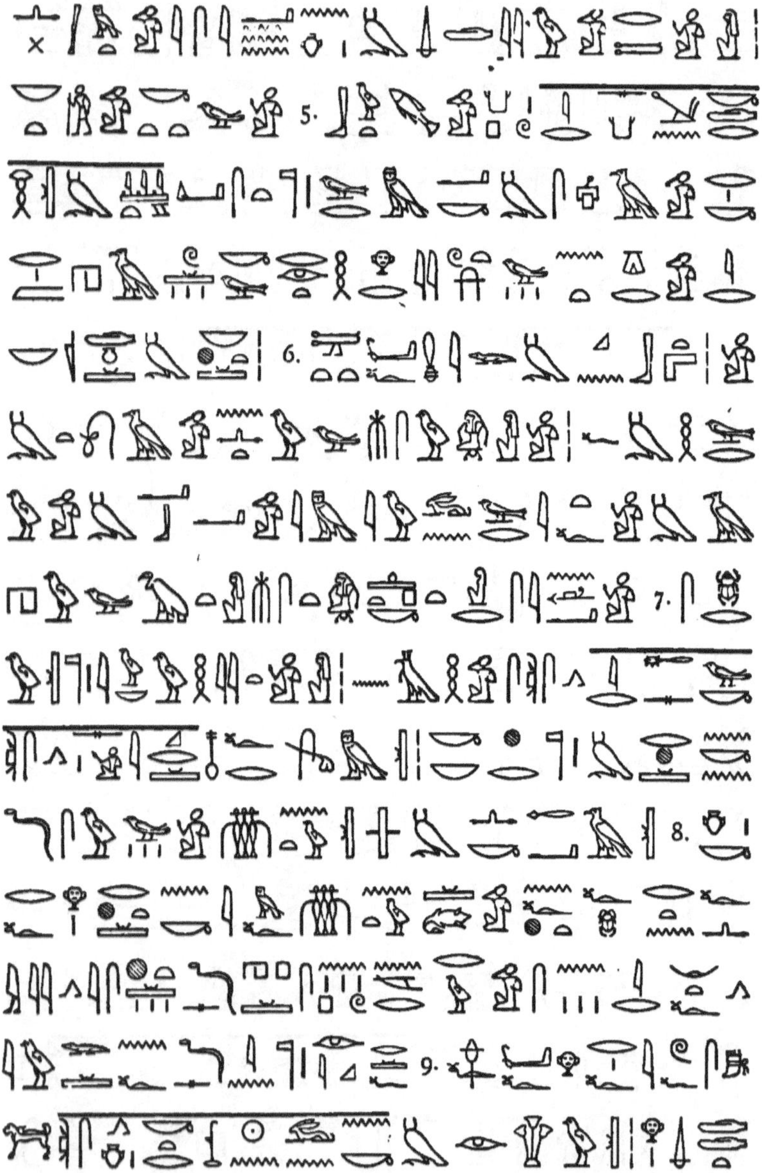
5.
6.
7.
8.
9.
10.

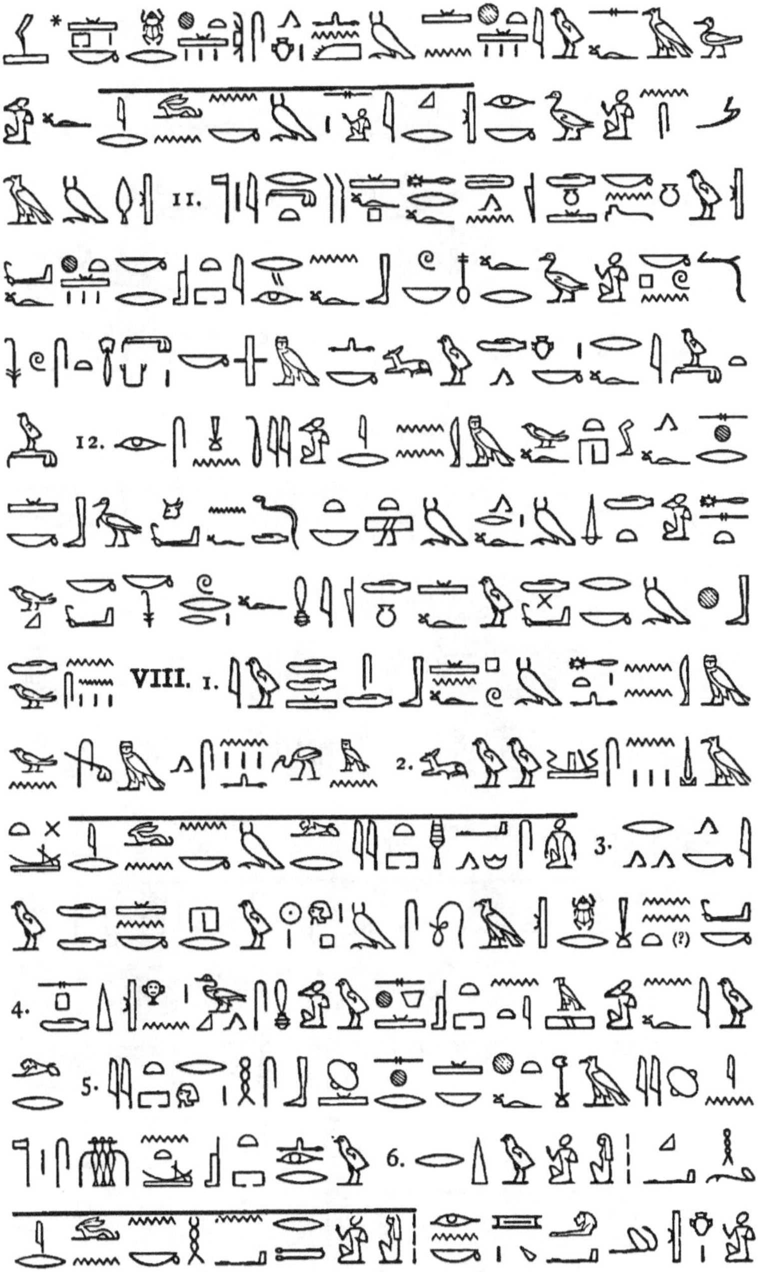

* The facsimile has [hieroglyph]

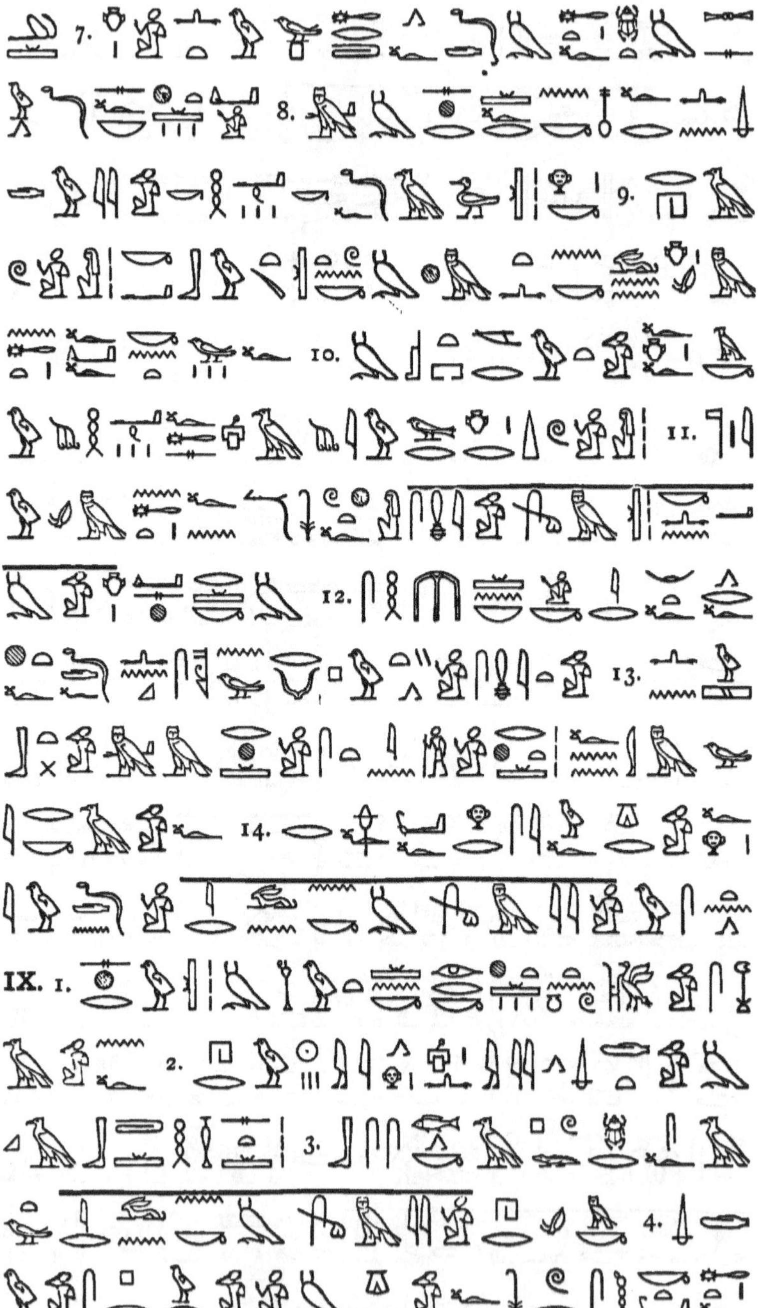
7.
8.
9.
10.
11.
12.
13.
14.
IX. 1.
2.
3.
4.

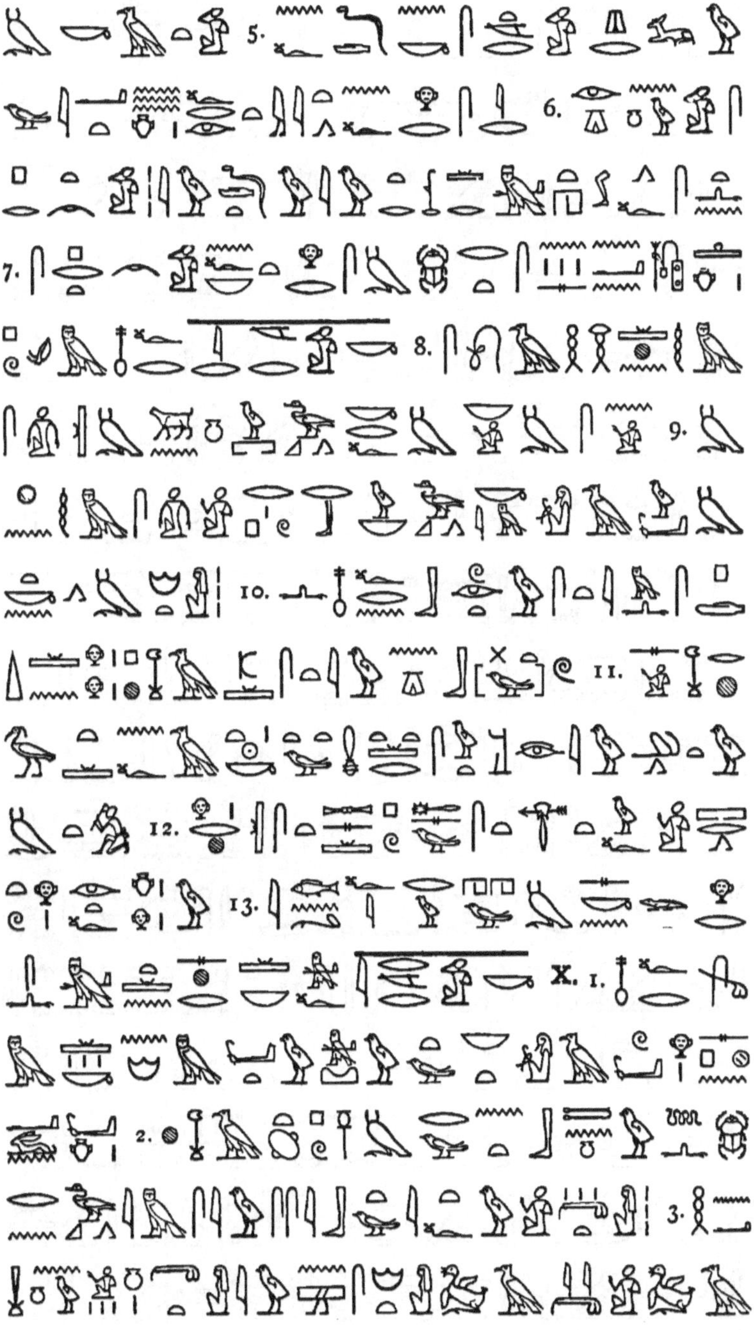

4.
5.
6.
7.
8.
9.
10.
11.
(?)
12.
XI. 1.
2.

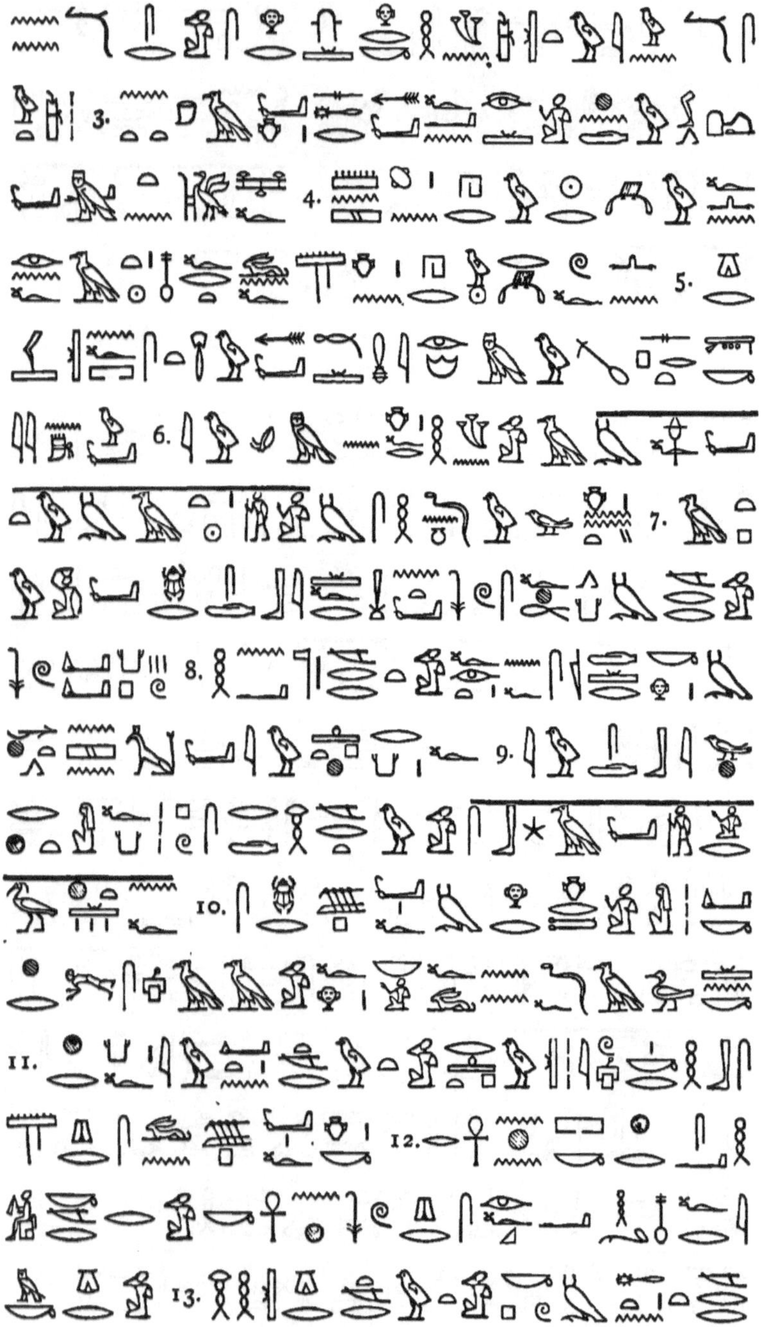
3.
4.
5.
6.
7.
8.
9.
10.
11.
12.
13.

XIII. 1.
2.
3.
(?)
4.
5.
6.
7.
8.
9.
10.
11.
12.
XIV. 1.
2.

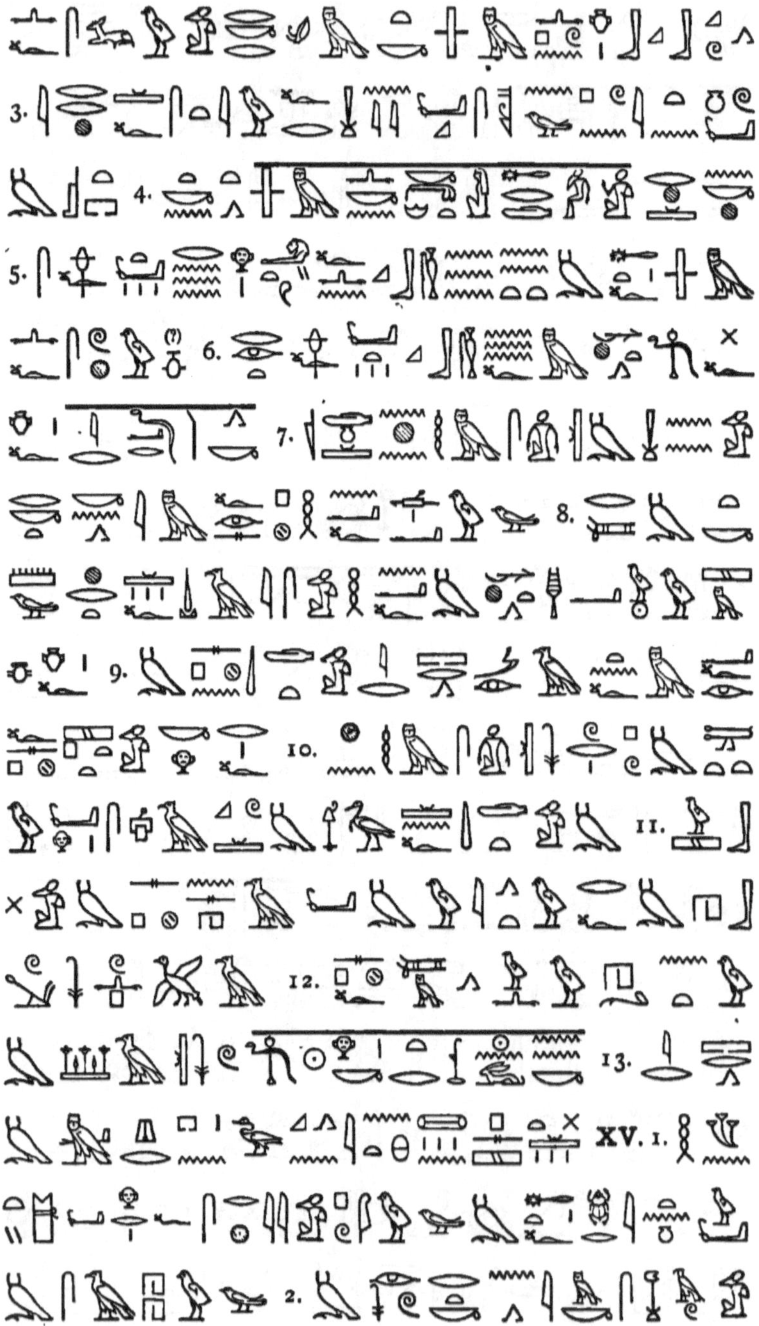

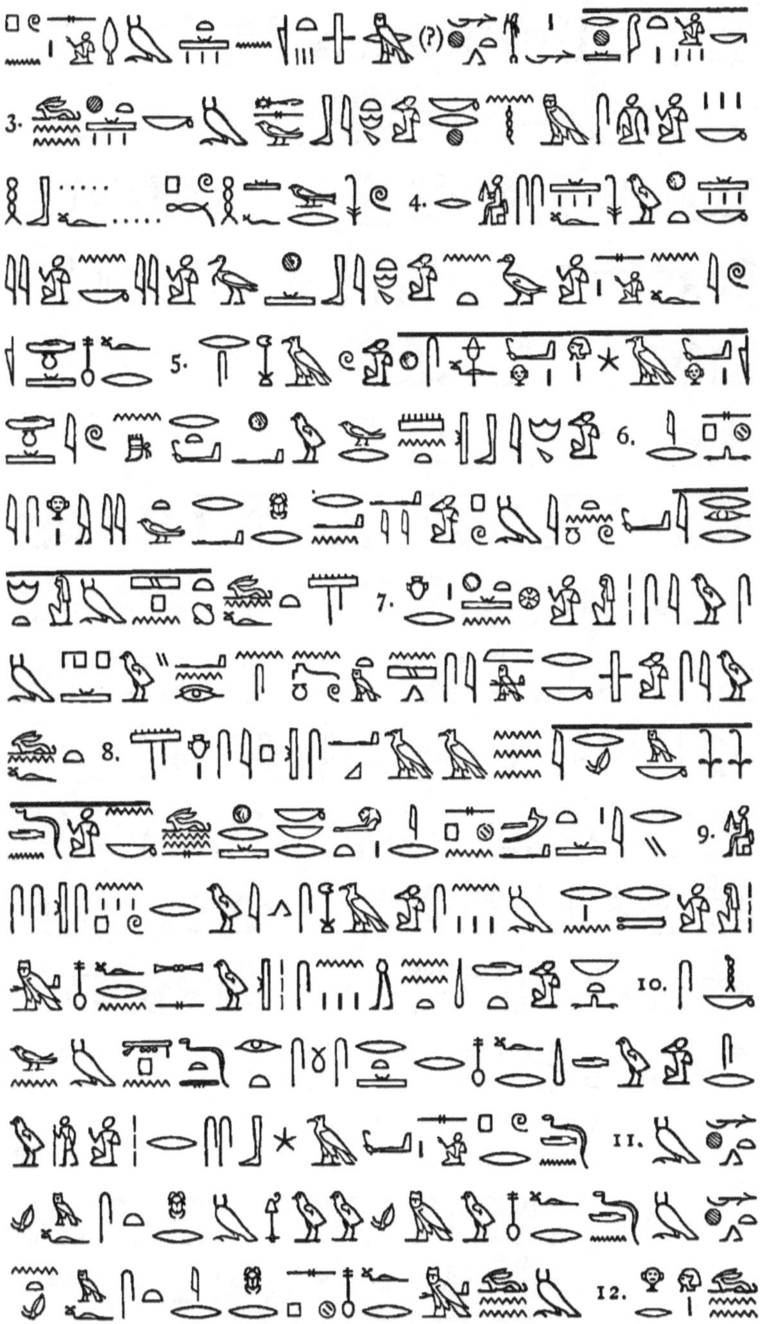

13.
XVI. 1.
2.
3.
4.
5.
6.
7.
8.
9.
10.
11.
12.

13.
14.
XVII. 1.
2.
3.
4.
5.
6.
7.
8.
9.
10.
11.
12.

XVIII. 1.
2.
3.
4.
5.
6.
7.
8.
9.
10.
11.
12.
13.
14.
XIX. 1.
2.
3.

THE TRAVELS OF AN EGYPTIAN.

XVIII.

5.
6.
7.
8.
XIX. 1.
2
3.
4.

5.
6.
7.
8.
9.
XX. 1.
2.
3.

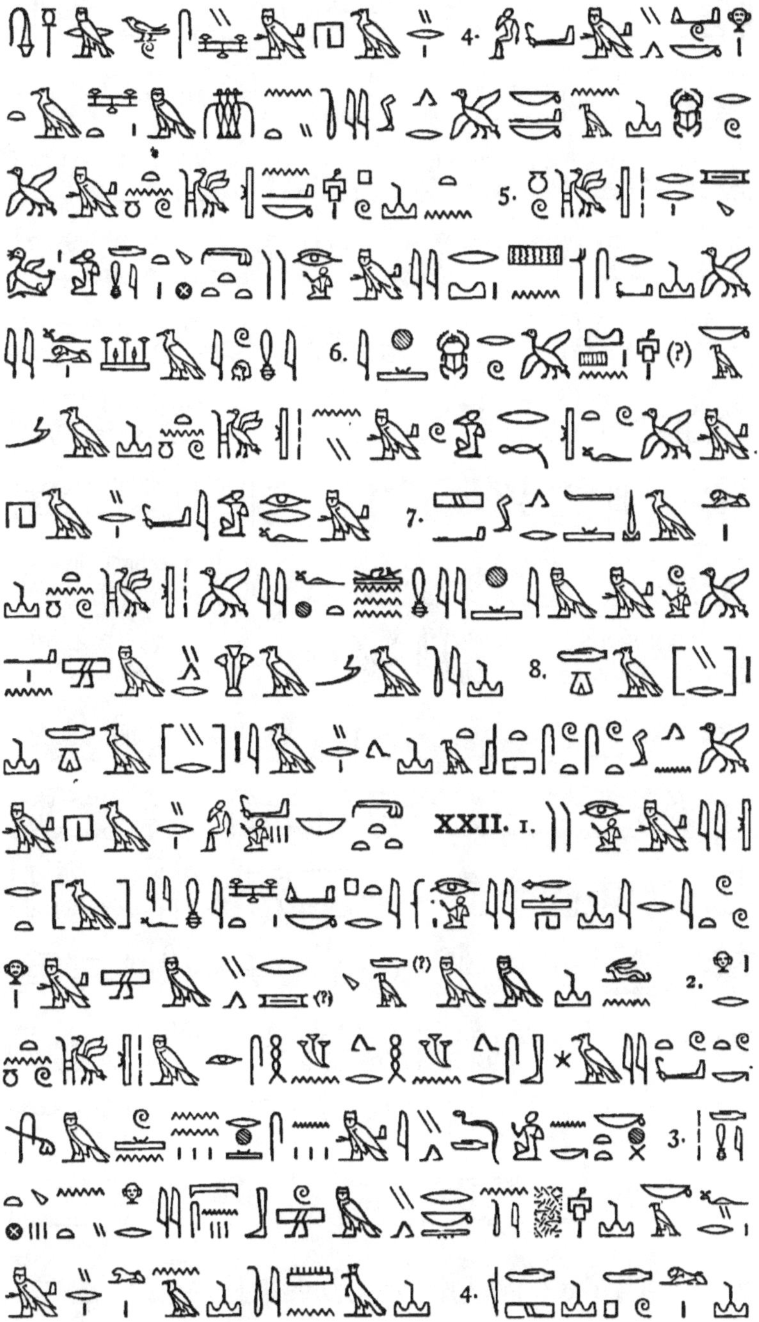
4.
5.
6.
(?)
7.
8.
XXII. 1.
(?)
(?)
2.
3.
4.

5.
6.
7.
8.
9.
XXIV. 1.
2.
(?)
(?)

3.
4.
5.
6.
7.
8.
XXV. 1.

2.
3.
4.
5.
6.
7.
8.
9.
XXVI. 1.

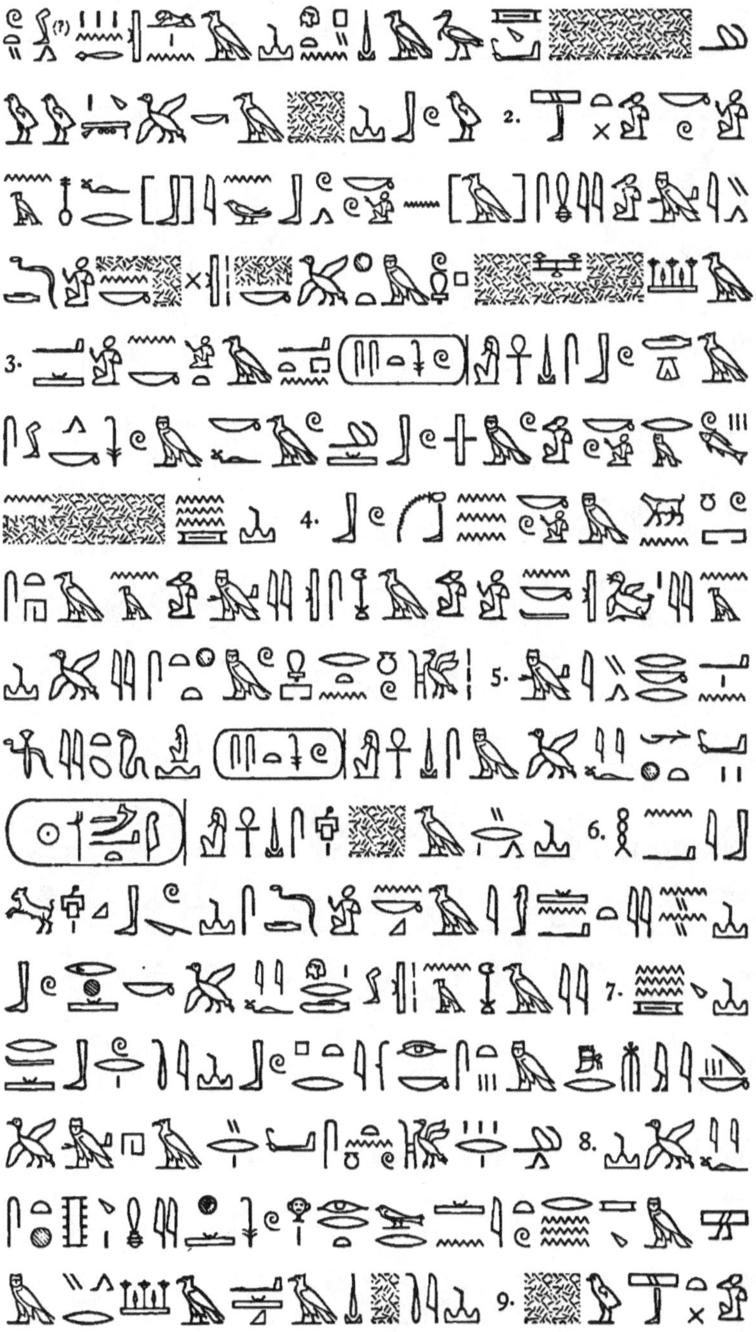

XXVIII. 1.
2.
3.
4.
5.

HYMN TO ÅMEN-RĀ.

* In the papyrus the dots are written in red ink.

II.

* Restored from Plate V, line 5.

V.

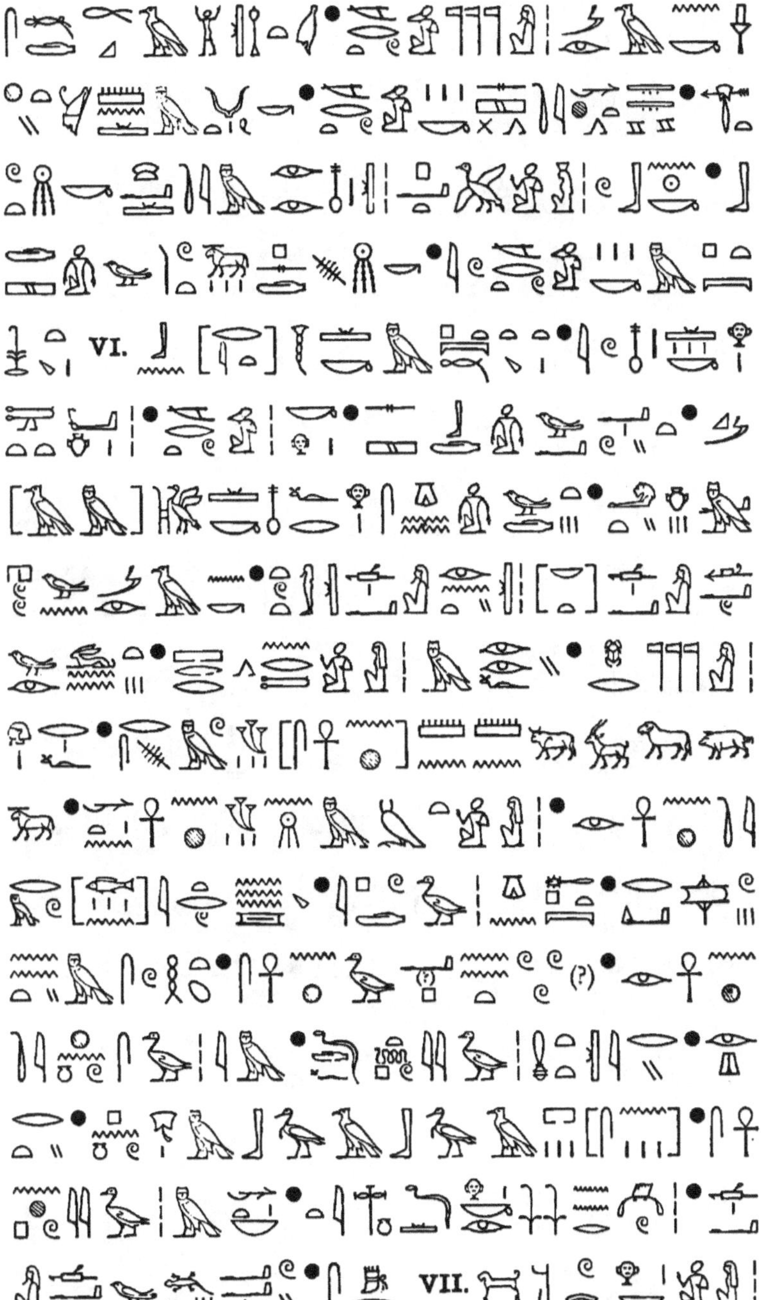
VI.
(?)
VII.

VIII.

IX.
X.

XI.

THE SPOLIATION OF THE TOMBS.

7.
8.
9.
10.
11.
3 inches broken.
12.
3 inches broken.
13.
3 inches broken.
14.
4 inches broken.
15.
16.
17.
18.
19.
(?)
20.
II. 1.

11.
12.
13.
14.
15.
16.
17.
18.
III. 1.

11.
12.
13.
14.
15.
16.
17.
18.
IV. 1.

14.
15.
16.
17.
18.
19.

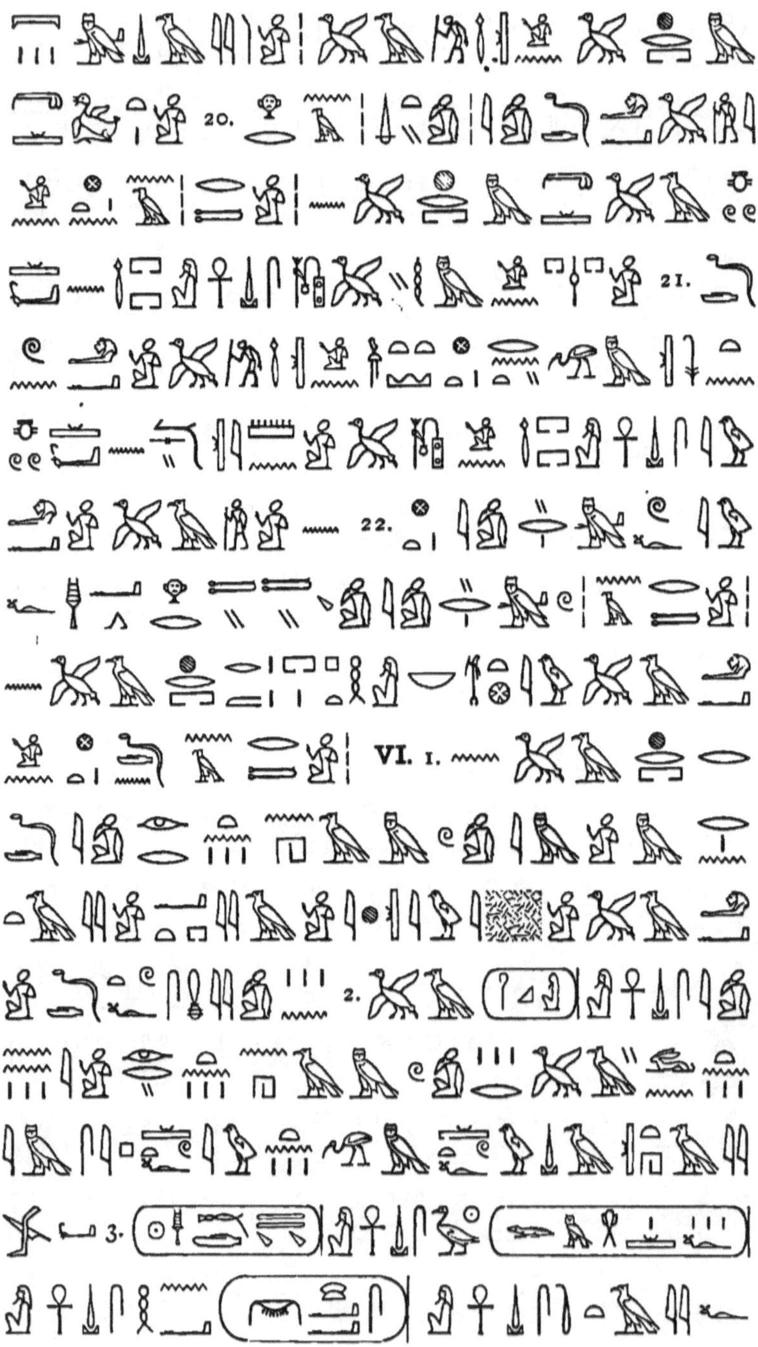
20.
21.
22.
VI. 1.
2.
3.

4.
5.
6.
7.
8.
9.
10.

2 inches broken
11.
12.
13.
14.
15.
16.

24.
VII. 1.
2.
3.
4.
5.
6.

7.
8.
9.
10.
11.
12.

HARRISON AND SONS, PRINTERS IN ORDINARY TO HER MAJESTY, ST. MARTIN'S LANE, LONDON.

www.ingramcontent.com/pod-product-compliance
Lightning Source LLC
Chambersburg PA
CBHW020907230426
43666CB00008B/1347